# The Greatest Gift

# The Greatest Gift

Julie K. Hogan, Editor

IDEALS PUBLICATIONS
NASHVILLE, TENNESSEE

ISBN 0-8249-5849-7
Published by Ideals Publications
A division of Guideposts
535 Metroplex Drive Suite 250
Nashville, Tennessee 37211
www.idealsbooks.com

Printed and bound in U.S.A. by R.R. Donnelley

Publisher, Patricia A. Pingry
Art Director, Eve DeGrie
Managing Editor, Peggy Schaefer
Production Manager, Travis Rader
Designer, Marisa Calvin
Copy Editor, Lisa Ragan
Permissions, Patsy Jay
Book Editor, Julie K. Hogan
Editorial Assistant, Margaret A. Hogan
Research Assistant, Mary P. Dunn

Library of Congress CIP data on file

Color scans by Precision Color Graphics, Franklin, Wisconsin

10 9 8 7 6 5 4 3 2 1

ACKNOWLEDGMENTS

BALDWIN, FAITH. "Christmas Is in the Unexpected Gift" from *Many Windows, Seasons of the Heart.* Copyright © 1958 by Faith Baldwin Cuthrell. "Christmas" from *The Christian Herald,* December 1949. Used by permission of Harold Ober Associates. *(Acknowledgments continued on page 160.)*

# The Greatest Gift

# CHRISTMAS-GIVING AND CHRISTMAS-LIVING

Henry Van Dyke

The custom of exchanging presents on a certain day in the year is very much older than Christmas and means very much less. It has been obtained in almost all ages of the world and among many different nations. It is a fine thing or a foolish thing, as the case may be; an encouragement to friendliness or a tribute to fashion; an expression of good nature or a bid for favor; an outgoing of generosity or a disguise of greed; a cheerful old custom or a futile old farce, according to the spirit which animates it and the form which it takes.

But when this ancient and variously interpreted tradition of a day of gifts was transferred to the Christmas season, it was brought into vital contact with an idea which must transform it, and with an example which must lift it up to a higher plane. The example is the life of Jesus. The idea is unselfish interest in the happiness of others.

Not that it must all be solemn and serious. For the most part it deals with little wants, little joys, little tokens of friendly feeling. But the feeling must be more than the token; else the gift does not really belong to Christmas.

It takes time and effort and unselfish expenditure of strength to make gifts in this way. But it is the only way that fits the season.

The finest Christmas gift is not the one that costs the most money but the one that carries the most love. . . .

But how seldom Christmas comes—only once a year; and how soon it is over—a night and a day! If that is the whole of it, it seems not much more durable than the little toys that one buys of a fakir on the street corner. They run for an hour and then the spring breaks and the legs come off, and nothing remains but a contribution to the dust heap.

But surely that need not and ought not to be the whole of Christmas. . . . If every gift is the token of a personal thought, a friendly feeling, an unselfish interest in the joy of others, then the thought, the feeling, the interest, may remain after the gift is made.

The little present, or the rare and long-wished-for gift . . . may carry a message something like this:

"I am thinking of you today, because it is Christmas, and I wish you happiness. And tomorrow, because it will be the day after Christmas, I shall still wish you happiness; and so on, clear through the year. I may not be able to tell you about it every day, because I may be far away; or because both of us may be very busy; or perhaps because I cannot even afford to pay the postage on so many letters or find the time to write them. But that makes no difference. The thought and the wish will be here just the same. In my work and in the business of life, I mean to try not to be unfair to you or injure you in any way. In my pleasure, if we can be together, I would like to share the fun with you. Whatever joy or success comes to you will make me glad. Without pretense, and in plain words, goodwill to you is what I mean, in the Spirit of Christmas."

It is not necessary to put a message like this into high-flown language, to swear absolute devotion and deathless consecration. In love and friendship, small, steady payments on a gold basis are better than immense promissory notes. Nor, indeed, is it always necessary to put the message into words at all, nor even to convey it by a tangible token. To feel it and to act it out—that is the main thing.

There are a great many people in the world whom we know more or less, but to whom for various reasons we cannot very well send a Christmas gift. But there is hardly one, in all the circles of our acquaintance, with whom we may not exchange the touch of Christmas life.

In the outer circles, cheerful greetings, courtesy, consideration; in the inner circles, sympathetic interest, hearty congratulations, honest encouragement; in the inmost circle, comradeship, helpfulness, tenderness.

> Beautiful friendship tried by sun and wind
> Durable from the daily dust of life.

After all, Christmas-living is the best kind of Christmas-giving.

# Everywhere, Everywhere, Christmas Tonight

Phillips Brooks

Everywhere, everywhere, Christmas tonight!
Christmas in lands of the fir-tree and pine,
Christmas in lands of the palm-tree and vine,
Christmas where snow peaks stand solemn and white,
Christmas where cornfields stand sunny and bright.

Christmas where children are hopeful and gay,
Christmas where old men are patient and gray,
Christmas where peace, like a dove in his flight,
Broods o'er brave men in the thick of the fight;
Everywhere, everywhere, Christmas tonight!

For the Christ-child who comes is the Master of all;
No palace too great, no cottage too small;
The angels who welcome Him sing from the height,
"In the city of David, a King in His might."
Everywhere, everywhere, Christmas tonight!

Then let every heart keep its Christmas within,
Christ's pity for sorrow, Christ's hatred for sin,
Christ's care for the weakest, Christ's courage for right,
Christ's dread of the darkness, Christ's love of the light.
Everywhere, everywhere, Christmas tonight!

So all the stars of the midnight which compass us round
Shall see a strange glory and hear a strange sound,
And cry, "Look! the earth is aflame with delight,
O sons of the morning, rejoice at the sight."
Everywhere, everywhere, Christmas tonight!

*The chimneys of peace on the roofs of snow keep watch, and the world is still.* —Esther M. Wood

# CHRISTMAS AND PETER MOSS

Mary Small

The waste ground close to the water's edge belonged to the Harbour Trust. Except for the gulls, it was no good for anything.

Nearby, partly hidden by trees, stood a small stone cottage. Peter Moss lived there. Once he had been a ship's engineer and had traveled all over the world . . . a long time ago.

The cottage was old, much older than Peter Moss. His grandfather had built it back in the early days. Many times the council had tried to buy it to make way for new buildings, but it was not for sale. Peter Moss often wondered what would happen to it when he died. He had no family, only Bosun, his dog.

Every day, Peter Moss and Bosun walked down to the waste ground for exercise. Bosun was young and full of energy. He loved to chase the stones and sticks that his master threw for him. When the old man grew tired, he would stand leaning on his stick gazing across the water to the tall, skyscraper buildings of the city. Sometimes a container ship would pass on its way to the docks and there were always ferries coming and going. Peter Moss reckoned

that he had the best view in the city. Yet, in spite of the bustle around him, he was lonely.

Every other day, except Sunday, Peter Moss made the long, slow walk to the shops at the top of Clark Street to buy groceries. It always alarmed him to see the bulldozers busy so near to his home and more and more flats rising up to the sky, full of new people. No one took any notice of the old man; they were too busy, too worried about their own affairs.

"Christmas gets earlier and earlier every year!" Peter Moss muttered as he looked in the shop windows. It was the time of the year he dreaded the most, for he was a shy man and although he had money, it could not buy him friends.

One Saturday morning he was surprised to see three youngsters with bikes walking around the waste ground talking together. They stayed there a long time and then went away.

On Sunday, more children came. They seemed very excited about something. They took spades and started to dig up the ground. Peter Moss stood at the window watching. He didn't like to interfere but they had no right to intrude. He waited a while, then opened the door and walked down with Bosun.

"What are you doing?" he asked. "This land belongs to the Harbour

Trust. You can't dig it up like that."

"Why not?" said Glen, the biggest boy. "It's not used for anything."

"We need somewhere to ride our bikes," said Nikos.

"The street's no good," said Werner, punching the ground with the heel of his boot.

"You'll get into big trouble if you do anything with it," said Peter Moss.

"But we want to make a practice track with dips and jumps," said Michelle. "For that we need rough ground. This couldn't be better."

All the youngsters stood and stared at him. Peter Moss didn't know what to do. "You'll have to find somewhere else," he said gruffly. Not wanting to argue, he called to Bosun and started to walk away. He could feel their strong resentment.

The youngsters muttered among themselves.

"There isn't anywhere!" shouted Glen angrily.

Peter Moss stopped. The children were right; for them there was nowhere. Youngsters nowadays didn't have the space he had when he was a boy.

"Watch it!" said Glen. "Old Nosey-Parker's coming back!"

Spades in their hands, they stood and waited.

"I've just had a thought," said Peter Moss. "I'm on the Harbour Trust Board Committee. You leave the ground alone and I'll have a talk to them and maybe to the council too."

"Okay by us," said Glen. "When will you know?"

"That I can't say," said Peter Moss. "You'll have to be patient. Come back and see me later this week. I live in the cottage up there."

The boys were at school when the people from the Harbour Trust came. They spent a long time looking at the land and a long time talking to Peter Moss. Then they went away. The old man felt sad. They hadn't made a decision, one way or the other. He knew that if the children didn't get the land they'd blame it on him and go elsewhere.

"This thing takes time," he said when the children knocked on the door.

Just when he had almost given up hope, the telephone rang. As Peter Moss listened to the voice, a big smile spread over his face.

"The kids will be delighted," he said. "Yes, I'll be only too pleased to keep an eye on things. I'm sure there'll be no trouble."

So the children dug ditches and made jumps and a track for their BMXs.

As the days grew longer, the old man had company most evenings and all the weekends. It was impossible for him to be lonely. When they weren't riding, the children would sit on the veranda and talk to him.

"When I was young, they didn't make bikes like that," said Peter Moss in amazement as Werner shot out from a ditch and twisted his bike in the air, and Nikos and Glen bounced over the Whoopy-doos.

"They're very expensive," said Elke. "Gino and Francesco who live next to us are selling newspapers to buy them."

"My brothers Jose and Mario are getting them for Christmas," said Rosa, "but you mustn't tell. It's a secret."

"Nikos hopes to trade his for a better one," said Sofie.

"No way can I get one," said Richard. "My dad's out of work."

"Nor I," said Paul. "We haven't the money."

From the conversations, Peter Moss was surprised that so many of the children living in the street came from different countries, places he knew quite well from his years at sea; Nikos and Sofie from Greece, Werner and Elke from Germany, Gino and Francesco from Italy, Jose, Mario, and Rosa from South America, Michelle from France, Danny and Kate from England. He heard about Tuan and Khai who had come from Vietnam in an open boat.

"They live over the shop next to the Chinese restaurant," said Kate. "They seem very poor and can't speak much English."

Peter Moss started to do a lot of thinking.

The Friday before Christmas, a white panel van pulled up at his house. When it had gone, Peter Moss went up the street to the hardware store. He bought a piece of shipboard, a small tin of paint and a brush. Then he went home and locked the door. He was busy all day.

Danny was the first to notice the sign hung on the veranda.

"Look!" he said, calling to the others. "BMX BIKES FOR HIRE, NO CHARGE. Say! What has the old man done?"

Dropping their bikes, the children raced up to the cottage and banged on the door. Bosun barked as Peter Moss opened it.

"Happy Christmas!" he said. "Come in and see!"

They crowded inside and there in a back room stood four brand new bikes.

"For anyone who needs one," said Peter Moss. "I asked for the best in the shop."

"They're sure good!" said Michelle. "Look, snake-belly tires, chrome-moly frames and all!"

Talking excitedly, the children jostled each other to hold the bikes.

"It's unreal!" said Glen. Thanks a million. Wait'll we tell the others."

Next evening, the children called a meeting at Werner's and Elke's house.

"What do you think he does at Christmastime?" they said.

"Probably nothing much."

On Christmas Eve, Peter Moss went to the shops early to buy food for himself and Bosun.

The waste ground lay silent and empty that evening. Peter Moss had just sat down to tea when Bosun growled softly. There was a noise of feet shuffling on the veranda, then suddenly voices started singing.

Peter Moss went to the door and opened it. There stood Nikos and Sofie and all their Greek friends. Peter Moss had never heard a song so beautiful.

"Happy Christmas, Mr. Moss!" sang out Rosa, and the carol singers moved aside so that her brothers Jose and Mario could carry a Christmas tree into the house. They placed it in a corner of the kitchen and the visitors crowded round, covering it with goodies and decorations.

"Our dad reckoned you'd need some good cheer," said Danny and Kate, putting a gift under the tree.

"And I bought a new collar for Bosun," said Richard.

"And I've brought him biscuits," said Paul.

"You must eat this tonight," said Elke, placing a cake braided and covered with icing on the table. "We call it a *stollen*. Gino and Francesco have some-

S.S.CARR.

thing for you too," and the Italian boys came forward with a dish full of delicious looking toffee.

"It's *torrone*," said Gino, "made from almonds and sugar and honey."

"You're invited to dinner at our place tomorrow," said Glen and Donna. "We'll fetch you at midday."

"We must hurry," said Rosa, "for we have our dinner tonight after church."

"We have ours too!" said Francesco.

Peter Moss sat down in his chair at the table. He looked at the children and the bright things around him. There were tears in his eyes.

"Thank you," he said very softly. "It's the most wonderful Christmas I've ever had."

# Good King Wenceslas

JOHN MASON NEALE

LATIN SPRING CAROL

1. Good King Wen - ces - las look'd out      On    the    Feast    of
2. "Hith - er,  page, and    stand   by   me,    If    thou know'st it
3. "Bring  me  flesh, and   bring me wine,    Bring  me   pine - logs
4. "Sire,     the  night is    dark - er  now,    And   the   wind blows
5. In       his  mas - ter's   steps  he   trod,    Where the   snow   lay

Ste   -   phen,        When  the   snow   lay        round     a - bout,
tell   -   ing,         Yon - der  peas - ant,        who     is       he?
hith  -   er,          Thou  and    I     will        see     him    dine,
strong -  er;          Fails  my   heart,   I         know   not    how,
dint  -   ed;          Heat  was    in    the         ver - y      sod

Deep and crisp and e - ven; Bright-ly shone the moon that night,
Where and what his dwell-ing?" "Sire, he lives a good league hence,
When we bear them thith-er." Page and mon-arch forth they went,
I can go no long-er." "Mark my foot-steps, my good page,
Which the saint had print-ed. There-fore, Chris-tian men, be sure,

Tho' the frost was cru - el, When a poor man
Un - der-neath the moun-tain; Right a - gainst the
Forth they went to - geth - er; Through the rude winds'
Tread thou in them bold-ly: Thou shalt find the
Wealth or rank pos - sess-ing, Ye who now will

came in sight, Gath - 'ring win - ter fu - el.
for - est fence, By Saint Ag - nes' foun - tain."
wild la - ment And the bit - ter weath - er.
win - ter's rage Freeze thy blood less cold - ly."
bless the poor, Shall your-selves find bless - ing.

# CAROLS IN THE COTSWOLDS

Laurie Lee

The week before Christmas, when snow seemed to lie thickest, was the moment for carol singing; and when I think back to those nights it is to the crunch of snow and to the lights of the lanterns on it. Carol singing in my village was a special tithe for the boys; the girls had little to do with it. Like haymaking, blackberrying, stone clearing, and wishing people a happy Easter, it was one of our seasonal perks.

So as soon as the wood had been stacked in the oven to dry for the morning fire, we put on our scarves and went out through the streets, calling loudly between our hands, till the various boys who knew the signal ran out from their houses to join us. One by one they came stumbling over the snow, swinging their lanterns round their heads, shouting and coughing horribly.

"Coming carol barking then?"

We were the Church Choir, so no answer was necessary. For a year we had praised the Lord out of key, and as a reward for this service we now had the right to visit all the big houses, to sing our carols and collect our tribute.

To work them all in meant a five-mile foot journey over wild and generally snowed-up country. So the first thing we did was to plan our route; a formality, as the route never changed. All the same, we blew on our fingers and argued; and then we chose our leader. This was not binding, for we all fancied ourselves as leaders, and he who started the night in that position usually trailed home with a bloody nose.

Eight of us set out that night. There was Sixpence the Simple, who had never sung in his life (he just worked his mouth in church); the brothers Horace and Boney, who were always fighting everybody and always getting the worst of it; Clergy Green, the preaching maniac; Walt the Bully; and my two brothers.

As we went down the lane other boys, from other villages, were already about the hills, bawling "Kingwenslush," and shouting through keyholes "Knock on the knocker! Ring at the bell! Give us a penny for singing so well!" They weren't an approved charity as we were, the choir; but competition was in the air.

Our first call as usual was the house of the Squire, and we trooped nervously down his drive. For light we had candles in marmalade jars suspended on loops of string, and they threw pale gleams on the towering snow-drifts that stood on each side of the drive. A blizzard was blowing but we were well wrapped up, with army puttees on our legs, woolen hats on our heads, and several scarves round our ears. As we approached the Big House across its white silent lawns, we too grew respectfully silent. The lake nearby was stiff and black, the waterfall frozen and still. We arranged ourselves shuffling round the big front door, then knocked and announced the choir.

A maid bore the tiding of our arrival away into the echoing distances of the house, and while we waited we cleared our throats noisily. Then she came back, and the door was left ajar for us, and we were bidden to begin. We brought no music; the carols were in our heads. "Let's give 'em 'Wild Shepherds',"said Jack. We began in confusion, plunging into a wreckage of keys, of different words and tempos; but we gathered our strength; he who sang loudest took the rest of us with him, and the carol took shape, if not sweetness.

This huge stone house, with its ivied walls, was always a mystery to us. What were those gables, those rooms and attics, those narrow windows veiled by the cedar trees? As we sang "Wild Shepherds" we craned our necks, gaping into the lamplit hall which we had never entered; staring at the muskets and untenanted chairs, the great tapestries furred by dust—until suddenly, on the stairs, we saw the old Squire himself standing and listening with his head on one side.

He didn't move until we'd finished; then slowly he tottered toward us, dropped two coins in our box with a trembling hand, scratched his name in the book we carried, gave us each a long look with his moist blind eyes, then turned away in silence. As though released from a spell we took a few sedate steps, then broke into a run for the gate. We didn't stop till we were out of the grounds. Impatient, at last, to discover the extent of his bounty, we squatted by the cow sheds, held our lanterns over the book, and saw that he had written "Two Shillings." This was quite a good start. No one of any worth in the district would dare to give us less than the Squire.

So with money in the box, we pushed on up the valley, pouring scorn on each other's performance. Confident now, we began to consider our quality and whether one carol was not better suited to us than another. Horace, Walt said, shouldn't sing at all; his voice was beginning to break.

Steadily we worked through the length of the valley, going from house to house, visiting the lesser and the greater gentry–the farmers, the doctors, the merchants, the majors, and other exalted persons. It was freezing hard and blowing too; yet not for a moment did we feel the cold. The snow blew into our faces, into our eyes and mouths, soaked through our puttees, got into our boots, and dripped from our woolen caps. But we did not care. The collecting box grew heavier, and the list of names in the book longer and more extravagant, each trying to outdo the other.

Mile after mile we went, fighting against the wind, falling into snowdrifts, and navigating by the lights of the houses. And yet we never saw our audience. We sang, as it were, at the castle walls.

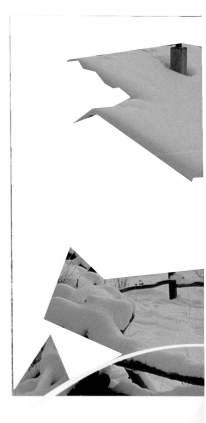

As the night drew on there was trouble with Boney. "Noel," for instance, had a rousing harmony which Boney persisted in singing, and singing flat. The others forbade him to sing it at all, and Boney said he would fight us. Picking himself up he agreed we were right, then he disappeared altogether. He just turned away and walked into the snow and wouldn't answer when we called him back. Much later, as we reached a far point up the valley, somebody said "Hark!" and we stopped to listen. Far away across the fields from the distant village came the sound of a frail voice singing, singing "Noel," and singing it flat—it was Boney, branching out on his own.

We approached our last house high up on the hill, the place of Joseph the farmer. For him we had chosen a special carol, which was about the other Joseph, so, that we always felt that singing it added a spicy cheek to the night. The last stretch of country to reach his farm was perhaps the most difficult of all. In these rough bare lanes, open to all winds, sheep were buried and wagons lost. Huddled together, we tramped in one another's footsteps, powdered snow blew into our screwed-up eyes, the candles burned low, some blew out altogether, and we talked loudly above the gale.

Crossing, at last, the frozen millstream—whose wheel in summer still turned a barren mechanism—we climbed up to Joseph's farm. Sheltered by trees, warm on its bed of snow, it seemed always to be like this. As always it was late; as always this was our final call. The snow had a fine crust upon it, and the old trees sparkled like tinsel. We grouped ourselves round the farmhouse porch. The sky cleared, and broad streams of stars ran down over the valley and away to Wales. On Slad's white slopes, seen through the black sticks of its woods, some red lamps still burned in the windows.

Everything was quiet; everywhere there was the faint crackling silence of

the winter night. We started singing, and we were all moved by the words and the sudden trueness of our voices. Pure, very clear, and breathless we sang:

> As Joseph was a-walking
> He heard an angel sing,
> 'This night shall be the birth-time
> Of Christ the Heavenly King.
> He neither shall be borned
> In Housen nor in hall,
> Nor in a place of paradise
> But in an ox's stall.'

And two thousand Christmases became real to us then; the houses, the halls, the places of paradise had all been visited; the stars were bright to guide the Kings through the snow; and across the farmyard we could hear the beasts in their stalls. We were given roast apples and hot mince pies, in our nostrils were spices like myrrh, and in our wooden box, as we headed back for the village, there were golden gifts for all.

*Each year, old carols are sung for a few. It's part of our gift beginning anew. The Christmas story never can end, for dear Jesus lives in the hearts of our friends.*
—*Author Unknown*

# Christmas Prayer
### Ralph Spaulding Cushman

Let not our hearts be busy inns
That have no room for Thee
But cradles for the living Christ
And His nativity.

Still driven by a thousand cares,
The pilgrims come and go;
The hurried caravans press on;
The inns are crowded so!

Here are the rich and busy ones,
With things that must be sold;
No room for simple things within
This hostelry of God.

Yet hunger dwells within these walls,
These shining walls and bright,
And blindness groping here and there
Without a ray of light.

Oh, lest we starve, and lest we die
In our stupidity,
Come, Holy Child, within and share
Our hospitality.

Let not our hearts be busy inns
That have no rooms for Thee
But cradles for the living Christ
And His nativity.

## The Joy of Christmas
John Greenleaf Whittier

Somehow, not only for Christmas
But all the year through,
The joy that you give to others
Is the joy that comes back to you;
And the more you spend in blessing
The poor and lonely and sad,
The more of your heart's possessing
Returns to make you glad.

## Let There Be Christmas
Author Unknown

So remember while December
Brings the only Christmas day,
In the year let there be Christmas
In the things you do and say.
Wouldn't life be worth the living,
Wouldn't dreams be coming true
If we kept the Christmas spirit
All the whole year through?

## Christmas Gifts
Alberta Dredla

Of all the gifts that Christmas brings,
The best are made of little things:
Melody of carols all the year;
Cheer to friends that you hold dear;
Courage to someone else to start
Some task for which he hasn't heart;
Thoughts for those with less than you;
Faith though the future's not in view;
Fun and laughter to go everywhere;
Kindness to show how much you care;
Strength to begin all over again;
And love to seek the best in every man.
While other seasons come and go
And another year hurries past,
Let's give again the little things—
They are the gifts that last.

Now not a window small or big
But wears a wreath or holly sprig.
—*Rachel Field*

# The Gift of an Open Door

# THE KEEPER OF THE INN

William P. Remington

There is an old story about the keeper of the inn, who owned the stable where Jesus was born. The census was being taken by Caesar Augustus; roads were crowded with people going to their own cities and the Inn at Bethlehem was full to overflowing. For one thing Marcus Publius, a great man of Rome with his servants and his horses, his scribes and his guards, filled the place. The old Innkeeper was kept hurrying hither and yon and even then could not do all the things demanded of him. And all the time more travelers were coming and asking that they might abide there for the night.

There was One who came the next morning, whom the Innkeeper would not have turned away for all the silver in the world, if only he had known who He was. There were two of them, a man, who might have been a carpenter or a potter, and his wife sitting all doubled up upon a donkey.

The man said his wife was ill and could travel no farther. But the Innkeeper grew angry at his pleas, shouting at him, "Can I make more rooms arise by striking my staff upon the ground?" And so the Innkeeper missed the greatest opportunity that ever an Innkeeper had. Long years afterwards it never did much good to repeat over and over again, "They were but poor folk and how was I to know?" When afterwards the Child Jesus was born in the stable and a great light filled all the heavens and there was a sound of heavenly music, Marcus Publius and his servants were still in a drunken sleep, and the Innkeeper had missed his great chance.

So it had been, and so it will be for many throughout the ages. Always there is that light in the heavens, that song in the air, that bright star, clear in the Eastern sky, which tell of the Birth of Christ. He comes to all and yet only a few see the light and run joyfully to the manger-cradled King.

We each one are the Keepers of the Inn. Never were there so many people on the roads demanding an entrance to our hearts and homes.

## You Merry Folk
### Geoffrey Smith

You merry folk, be of good cheer,
For Christmas comes but once a year.
From open door you'll take no harm
By winter if your hearts are warm.
So ope the door and hear us carol
The burthen of our Christmas moral.
Be ye merry and make good cheer,
For Christmas comes but once a year;
Scrape the fiddle and beat the drum,
And bury the night ere morning come.

## Home for Christmas
### Minnie Klemme

The folks are coming home for Christmas.
All the windows are aglow;
We have a tree and wreaths and candles,
And we have some snow!

There are gifts upon the mantel
And there are gifts beneath the tree;
The whole house is breathing Christmas
And so by now are we.

Do I hear sleigh bells in the distance?
We're waiting from cellar to dome.
Hurrah, hurrah, a merry Christmas—
The folks are finally home!

*We gathered all our packages and climbed aboard the train, and off to Grandmama's we went at Christmastime again.* —Marguerite Gode

# THE FIR TREE

Hans Christian Andersen

*M*ost children have seen a Christmas tree, and many know that the pretty and pleasant custom of hanging gifts on its boughs comes from Germany; but perhaps few have heard or read the story that is told to little German children, respecting the origin of this custom. The story is called "The Little Stranger" and runs thus: In a small cottage on the borders of a forest lived a poor laborer, who gained a scanty living by cutting wood. He had a wife and two children who helped him in his work. The boy's name was Valentine, and the girl was called Mary. They were obedient, good children, and a great comfort to their parents. One winter evening, this happy little family was sitting quietly round the hearth, the snow and the wind raging outside, while they ate their supper of dry bread, when a gentle tap was heard on the window, and a childish voice cried from without, "Oh, let me in, pray! I am a poor child with nothing to eat and no home to go to, and I shall die of cold and hunger unless you let me in."

Valentine and Mary jumped up from the table and ran to open the door, saying, "Come in, poor little child! We have not much to give you, but whatever we have we will share with you."

The stranger-child came in and warmed his frozen hands and feet at the fire, and the children gave him the best they had to eat, saying, "You must be tired, too, poor child! Lie down on our bed; we can sleep on the bench for one night."

Then said the little stranger-child, "Thank God for all your kindness to me!" So they took their little guest into their sleeping-room, laid him on the bed, covered him over, and said to each other, "How thankful we ought to be! We have warm rooms and a cozy bed, while this poor child has only heaven for his roof and the cold earth for his sleeping-place."

When their father and mother went to bed, Mary and Valentine lay quite contentedly on the bench near the fire, saying, before they fell asleep, "The stranger-child will be so happy tonight in his warm bed!"

These kind children had not slept many hours before Mary awoke, and softly whispered to her brother, "Valentine, dear, wake and listen to the sweet music under the window."

*Christmas is not a time nor a season but a state of mind. To cherish peace and goodwill, to be plenteous in mercy, is to have the real spirit of Christmas.*
*—Calvin Coolidge*

Then Valentine rubbed his eyes and listened. It was sweet music indeed, and sounded like beautiful voices singing to the tones of a harp:

> O holy Child, we greet thee! bringing
> Sweet strains of harp to aid our singing.
> Thou, holy Child, in peace art sleeping,
> While we our watch without are keeping.
> Blest be the house wherein thou liest,
> Happiest on earth, to heaven the nighest.

The children listened, while a solemn joy filled their hearts; then they stepped softly to the window to see who might be without.

In the east was a streak of rosy dawn, and in its light they saw a group of children standing before the house, clothed, in silver garments, holding golden harps in their hands. Amazed at this sight, the children were still gazing out of the window when a light tap caused them to turn around. There stood the stranger-child before them, clad in a golden dress, with a gleaming radiance round his curling hair. "I am the little Christ child," he said, "who wanders through the world bringing peace and happiness to good children. You took me in and cared for me when you thought me a poor child, and now you shall have my blessing for what you have done."

A fir tree grew near the house; and from this he broke a twig, which he planted in the ground, saying, "This twig shall become a tree and shall bring forth fruit year by year for you."

No sooner had he done this than he vanished and with him the little choir of angels. But the fir-branch grew and became a Christmas tree, and on its branches hung golden apples and silver nuts every Christmastide.

Such is the story told to German children concerning their beautiful Christmas trees, though we know that the real little Christ child can never be wandering, cold and homeless, again in our world, inasmuch as he is safe in heaven by his Father's side; yet we may gather from this story the same truth which the Bible plainly tells us that anyone who helps a Christian child in distress, it will be counted unto him as if he had indeed done it unto Christ himself. "Inasmuch as ye have done it unto the least of these, my brethren, ye have done it unto me."

## As Ye Do It unto These

Author Unknown

In little faces pinched with cold and hunger
Look, lest ye miss Him! In the wistful eyes
And on the mouths unfed by mother kisses,
Marred, bruised, and stained, His precious image lies!
And when ye find Him in the midnight wild,
Even in the likeness of an outcast child,
O wise men, own your King!
Before His cradle bring
You gold to raise and bless,
Your myrrh of tenderness,
For "As ye do it unto these," said He,
"Ye do it unto Me."

## A Kindled Flame of Love

Edgar A. Guest

When it's Christmas, man is bigger
    And is better in his part;
He is keener for the service
    that is prompted by his heart.
All the petty thoughts and narrow
    seem to vanish for awhile
And the true reward he's seeking
    is the glory of a smile.
Then for others he is toiling
    and somehow it seems to me
That at Christmas he is almost
    what God wanted him to be.

*Christmas is the season for kindling the fire of hospitality in the hall, the genial flame of charity in the heart.*
—*Washington Irving*

# The Christmas Guest

Author Unknown

It happened one day near December's end,
Two neighbors called on an old-time friend,
And they found his shop so meager and mean,
Made gay with a thousand boughs of green.
And Conrad was sitting with face a-shine
When he suddenly stopped as he stitched a twine.

And said, "Old friends, at dawn today
When the cock was crowing the night away,
The Lord appeared in a dream to me
And said, 'I am coming your guest to be.'
So I've been busy with feet astir
Strewing my shop with branches of fir.

The table is spread and the kettle is shined
And over the rafters the holly is twined.
And now I will wait for my Lord to appear
And listen closely so I will hear
His step as he nears my humble place
And I open the door and look on his face."

So his friends went home and left Conrad alone,
For this was the happiest day he had known.
For long since his family had passed away
And Conrad had spent many a sad Christmas Day.
But he knew with the Lord as his Christmas guest,
This Christmas would be the dearest and best.

So he listened with only joy in his heart,
And with every sound he would rise with a start
And look for the Lord to be at the door
Like the vision he had a few hours before.
So he ran to the window after hearing a sound,
But all he could see on the snow-covered ground

Was a shabby beggar whose shoes were torn
And all of his clothes were ragged and worn;
But Conrad was touched and went to the door,
And he said, "Your feet must be frozen and sore—
I have some shoes in my shop for you,
And a coat that will keep you warmer, too."

So with grateful heart the man went away,
But Conrad noticed the time of day;
He wondered what made the dear Lord so late
And how much longer he'd have to wait
When he heard a knock and ran to the door,
But it was only a stranger once more—

A bent old lady with a shawl of black,
With a bundle of kindling piled on her back.
She asked for only a place to rest
But that was reserved for Conrad's great guest,
But her voice seemed to plead, "Don't send me away,
Let me rest for a while on Christmas Day."

So Conrad brewed her a steaming cup
And told her to sit at the table and sup.
But after she left, he was filled with dismay,
For he saw that the hours were slipping away,
And the Lord had not come as he said he would
And Conrad felt sure he had misunderstood.

When out of the stillness he heard a cry,
"Please help me and tell me where am I."
So again he opened his friendly door
And stood disappointed as twice before.
It was only a child who had wandered away
And was lost from her family on Christmas Day.

Again Conrad's heart was heavy and sad
But he knew he could make this little girl glad.
So he called her in and wiped her tears
And quieted all her childish fears,
Then he led her back to her home once more,
But as he entered his own darkened door,

He knew that the Lord was not coming today
For the hours of Christmas had passed away.
So he went to his room and knelt down to pray,
And he said, "Lord, why did you delay,
What kept you from coming to call on me,
For I wanted so much your face to see."

When soft in the silence, a voice he heard,
"Lift up your head for I kept my word.
Three times my shadow crossed your floor,
Three times I came to your lowly door;
For I was the beggar with bruised cold feet;
I was the woman you gave something to eat,

And I was the child on the homeless street.
Three times I knocked, three times I came in,
And each time I found the warmth of a friend.
Of all the gifts, love is the best;
I was honored to be your Christmas Guest."

# God Rest Ye Merry, Gentlemen

TRADITIONAL ENGLISH

1. God rest ye mer - ry, gen-tle-men, Let noth-ing you dis - may,
2. From God our Heav'n-ly Fa - ther, A bless-ed an-gel came;
3. "Fear not,then," said the an - gel, "Let noth-ing you af - fright,
4. The shep-herds at those ti - dings Re - joic-ed much in mind,
5. And when they came to Beth-le-hem Where our dear Sav-iour lay,

Re - mem-ber Christ our Sav - iour Was born on Christ-mas day,
And un - to cer - tain shep - herds Bro't ti-dings of the same:
This day is born a Sav - iour Of a pure Vir - gin bright,
And left their flocks a - feed - ing, In tem-pest,storm and wind:
They found Him in a man - ger, Where ox - en feed on hay;

To   save   us   all   from   Sa - tan's pow'r,   When we were gone a - stray.
How   that   in Beth - le - hem   was born   The Son   of   God by name.
To   free   all those who   trust   in   Him   From Sa - tan's pow'r and might."
And   went to Beth - le - hem straight - way,   The Son   of   God to   find.
His   moth - er   Ma - ry   kneel - ing   down,   Un - to the Lord did   pray.

O   ti - dings of   com — fort and   joy, com - fort and

joy,   O   ti — dings of   com — fort and   joy.

# THE TAILOR'S CHRISTMAS GUEST

Marcel Brun and Betty Bowen

Hundreds of years ago, when the hilltops of Northern France bristled with the turrets and battlements of great feudal castles, there lived a rich and handsome aristocrat named Gilbert de Maupertuis. In Lord Gilbert's castle, with its high donjon and its walls shining with arms and trophies, were a lively group of fashionable lords and ladies who lived only to amuse themselves, from sunrise to midnight, in an endless diversity of sports and pastimes.

Almost every day twenty stalwart knights, led by Gilbert himself, spurred their horses over the chateau's stout drawbridge and down the hill, their bright plumes and banners dancing and skipping about like the people of Avignon. Some mornings, accompanied by their giant mastiffs, they hunted; often they rode out to try their skill at some tournament given by a neighboring lord; just as often they galloped across the fields to storm the castle of a hostile nobleman.

Renowned Gilbert spurned no opportunity to gain even greater glory. Indeed, it was whispered that he sometimes waged war for no cause whatever.

So great was the reputation of this gentleman and his knights for reckless daring that his enemies no longer deemed it cowardly to hastily retire behind their moats when they saw his banners approaching; rather it was thought prudent and wise.

Each day at sundown, tired but exhilarated, the heroes would return to Maupertuis to enjoy their customary evening of merriment and gaiety and to charm the ladies with their thrilling stories of adventure.

All was not happy-go-lucky mirth and gaiety among the tenants who lived in the little village below the castle. Often their fields were ravaged by brigandeering knights; sometimes their crops were destroyed and they were forced to live in dire poverty with barely enough food to keep themselves alive through the winter months. They could bake their bread only in their master's ovens. They must marry whom their lord suggested. They must be forever willing to be called to his service. If they tried to escape or dared to complain about their wretchedness, Lord Gilbert made his exactions even more rigid. Life in the village was very hard.

In fact, if it had not been for the good tailor, many of the commoners could not have survived. Old Jacquet was the only peasant on the manor toward whom Gilbert de Maupertuis showed any kindness at all. It was he who fashioned the fine clothes which were so important in gaining distinction for oneself. Indeed, Lord Gilbert de Maupertuis was sometimes called the most gorgeously dressed gentleman of all Western Europe. Jacquet was indispensable.

With the utmost humbleness, the tailor would venture to ask little favors of his master, never selfishly, but always for those less fortunate than himself. He was the only one who could obtain the noble's occasional goodwill.

The great man used to visit his tailor often for fittings, and as Jacquet worked, he would amuse himself by shocking the poor old man with his blasphemous stories about the wickedness and impiety of the priests and the bishops and the archbishops. Poor Jacquet used to dread seeing Lord Gilbert after the nobleman and his knights had won a battle, or after he had jousted some unfortunate peer in a tournament.

Jacquet was an exceedingly pious man, and exaltation lent to the lord's mockery an almost unbearable keenness. "How strange it seems that the great King of Heaven, who has power over all mankind, was unable to save the Holy Land from the infidels!" proud Gilbert would exclaim. Many, many times after his master had criticized the priests and the monks and the pope and even Christ or God himself, the poor old tailor would pray, begging the saints to remove the veil from his master's eyes so that he too might feel God's divine presence.

One day the good tailor told his seigneur a little story: "My Lord," he said, "Many years ago, Jesus returned to earth. Dressed in beggar's rags, he went from door to door to beg alms. The folk who received him well he blessed, and they lived afterwards in great happiness. But upon the heads of those who turned him away, Jesus placed a solemn malediction, and ever afterwards they knew only darkness and despair."

Of course, Lord Gilbert only laughed disrespectfully and mocked poor Jacquet. "Well," he said, with playful mercilessness, "if Jesus knocks at your door, I shall be willing to give him the most handsome suit of clothes you can make!"

Now it happened that His Majesty, King Philip, desiring to hear the holy mass of Christmas Eve at the famous Rheims Cathedral, sent a messenger to Lord Gilbert asking him for the night's lodging in his castle. His lordship felt extremely joyful and proud that such a great honor should be bestowed upon him.

In haste he cantered down the hill to his tailor's workshop to order the most splendid costume Jacquet could make. For almost an hour Lord Gilbert fingered and examined samples of costly velvets and satins of endless varieties, and finally decided that he would appear the most dashing in flaming red brocade. My, but it was going to be elegant! It was to be very snugly fitted, lined with pearly satin as soft as swan's-down, trimmed with luscious, rich ermine. The crowning touch was to be a mountainous ruff of Flemish lace, delicately fluted according to the latest style.

Jacquet had just two weeks to finish his master's beautiful Christmas suit. Hour after hour his diligent fingers busied themselves with cutting and stitching, hemming and pressing. Even late at night, lamplight peeked out from his shaded windows, which lent an air of mystery to this modest peasant so hard at work. The commoners decided that their kind friend was surely hiding something from them, and the buzz of gossip and speculation grew louder and louder during those busy days before Christmas. What could he be making?

When Christmas Eve came, Jacquet helped his liege to don his new suit of clothes at his shop. A cluster of townspeople loitered about the door in anticipation. Jacquet heeded every particular, even to a careful sprinkling with costly Oriental perfume. The folk of the town, catching glimpses of scarlet and white inside, sniffed the air appreciatively.

Just as Lord Gilbert was leaving, Jacquet said quietly, "My Lord, I have something to announce to you. Jesus has knocked at my door. I have done as you said I should; I have given Jesus the finest suit of clothes I could make." Then the tailor pulled aside the curtain to his back room. There stood a

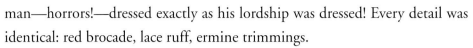

man—horrors!—dressed exactly as his lordship was dressed! Every detail was identical: red brocade, lace ruff, ermine trimmings.

Lord Gilbert de Maupertuis drew nearer. In dreadful fascination he gazed at this other glorious aristocrat—and recognized the poor rascal who begged alms near the gates of his castle. The men and women whispered and snorted with glee to see the richly dressed twins.

Suddenly, turning purple with rage, Gilbert seized his tailor by the shoulder. Jacquet felt no fear for himself—no, not even when his master raised a brocaded arm to box his ears. He stood very still, and only his eyes betrayed his soul, which was fervently praying, "Blessed Saint Peter, please, please. Help him to see Jesus!"

Something very strange happened. Lord Gilbert's arm dropped to his side; and as he turned away, it seemed as though a part of Jacquet's quiet patience had passed into his heart as well. "All right, I'll pay for it," he said slowly. Then he hustled out to his horse muttering, "Jesus! Jesus in that scamp of a beggar! Who could believe such a thing?"

So great was his preoccupation that Lord Gilbert was hardly aware of climbing to his saddle. As he rode along, his anger melted away completely, and all his efforts to call it back were in vain.

All of a sudden, halfway up the hill, as he looked up at the first Christmas Eve star, he understood why he felt so very meek and yet so sublimely happy. He knew he could never see, as Jacquet did, that the rascal who had come to the shop door to beg for bread was Jesus himself; but deep down in his heart a voice was whispering to him over and over again that the Spirit of Jesus had been there, had been in that room, not in the poor beggar's body, but in his good tailor's heart.

## Christmas Eve

Author Unknown

| | |
|---|---|
| The latch is on the door tonight, | My heart is open wide tonight, |
| The hearth fire is aglow; | For stranger, kith, or kin; |
| I seem to hear soft passing feet— | I would not bar a single door |
| The Christ Child in the snow. | Where love might enter in. |

## The Time Has Come

Poor Robin's Almanack

Now that the time has come wherein
Our Saviour Christ was born,
The larder's full of beef and pork,
The granary's full of corn.
As God hath plenty to thee sent,
Take comfort of thy labors,
And let it never thee repent,
To feast thy needy neighbors.

## Old Christmas Returned

Author Unknown

All you that to feasting and mirth are inclined,
Come here is good news  for to pleasure your mind,
Old Christmas is come for to keep open house,
He scorns to be guilty of starving a mouse:
Then come, boys, and welcome  for diet the chief,
Plum-pudding, goose, capon, minced pies, and roast beef.

The holly and ivy about the walls wind
And show that we ought to our neighbors be kind,
Inviting each other for past-time and sport,
And where we best fare, there we most do resort;
We fail not of victuals, and that of the chief,
Plum-pudding, goose, capon, minced pies, and roast beef.

All travellers, as they do pass on their way,
At gentlemen's halls are invited to stay,
Themselves to refresh, and their horses to rest,
Since that he must be Old Christmas's guest;
Nay, the poor shall not want, but have for relief,
Plum-pudding, goose, capon, minced pies, and roast beef.

# A Greeting of Love

Fra Giovanni

There is nothing I can give you which you have not; but there is much, very much that, while I cannot give it, you can take. No heaven can come to us unless our hearts find rest in today. Take heaven! No peace lies in the future which is not hidden in the present. Take peace!

The gloom of the world is but a shadow. Behind it, yet within our reach, is joy. Take joy! There is radiance and glory in the darkness could we but see, and to see, we have only to look. I beseech you to look.

Life is so generous a giver, but we, judging its gifts by the covering, cast them away as ugly, or heavy, or hard. Know the covering, and you will find beneath it, a living splendor, woven of love, by wisdom, with power.

And so, at this Christmas time, I greet you. Not quite as the world sends greetings, but with profound esteem and with the prayer that for you, now and forever, the day breaks and the shadows flee away.

# A Christmas Prayer

Robert Louis Stevenson

Loving Father, help us remember the birth of Jesus, that we may share in the song of the angels, the gladness of the shepherds, and the worship of the wise men. Close the door of hate and open the door of love all over the world. Let kindness come with every gift and good desires with every greeting. Deliver us from evil by the blessing which Christ brings and teach us to be merry with clear hearts. May the Christmas morning make us happy to be Thy children, and the Christmas evening bring us to our beds with grateful thoughts, forgiving and forgiven, for Jesus' sake. Amen!

# PRAYER AT CHRISTMAS

Pat Corrick Hinton

God our Father, it's Christmas at last. Thank you for this big celebration. We are happy because you have given us your greatest gift of love, Jesus your Son. We welcome Jesus and thank you for all the love and hope and peace He brings us. Help us to be like Jesus and bring love and hope and peace to each other. Let the love in our family reach out to everyone we meet today and tomorrow and every day.

*Christmas is a golden chain that binds a family in faith, hope, and love . . . drawing each to the open hearth of togetherness.*
—Juanita Johnson

## The Song and the Star

Grace V. Watkins

My father had the shining gift of song.
His voice was cello-beautiful and strong.
Oh, sometimes, listening to the choir where he
Gave humble, dedicated ministry,
I felt I stood with shepherds, hearing bright
Allegro anthems syllabled with light;
then came with gladness to the manger place
and looked upon the Christ Child's holy face.

My mother had the gift of quietness.
How often her tranquility would bless
My weariness with peace! And in her eyes
It often seemed I saw the star arise
In silent majesty so calm and fair
My heart was filled with wonderment of prayer,
As though that star, more lovely than a gem,
Were leading me to the Child of Bethlehem.

What sweet, what priceless memories they are:
The golden-echoing song, the quiet star!

# LATE FOR CHRISTMAS

Mary Ellen Chase

During those confusing days before Christmas, while I wrap gifts for sisters and brothers, brothers-in-law and sisters-in-law, nephews and nieces, aunts and great-aunts, neighbors and friends, the milkman, the postman, the paper boy, the cook and the cook's children, the cleaning woman and the cleaning woman's children, I remember my grandmother, who in the twenty years I knew her wrapped Christmas gifts for no one at all. My grandmother never stood half submerged in a jungle of silver cord, gold cord, red ribbon, tinsel ribbon, white tissue paper, red tissue paper, paper marked with Aberdeens or angels. She viewed with fine scorn all such pre-Christmas frenzy. I remember her again when my January bills weigh down my desk and my disposition. My grandmother in all those years never bought a Christmas gift for anyone, although she gave many. Nor did she make her Christmas gifts by the labor of her hands, which were almost never idle.

To be sure, she spent most of her waking hours during twelve months of the year in making gifts, but they were not for Christmas. She made yards upon yards of tatting, fashioned hundreds of tea cozies, tidies, and table mats,

hem-stitched innumerable handkerchiefs, crocheted fine filet for pillowcases and sheets, knit countless scalloped bands of white lace for the legs of white cotton drawers, and countless stockings, gloves, mittens, scarfs, sacques, and shawls. These creations were all gifts, yet they were never given at Christmas. Instead, they were presented at odd moments to all sorts of odd and sundry persons—to the gardener, the minister's wife, a surprised boy coasting down the hill, the village schoolmistresses, the stage driver, a chance Syrian peddler,

the fishman, the paperhangers, an unknown woman distributing religious literature at the back door, the sexton. Moreover, no one of my grandmother's many acquaintances ever called upon her without departing from her door richer, or at least more encumbered, than when she entered it—nor did my grandmother ever set out empty-handed to return those calls.

My grandmother's nature was essentially dramatic. She loved all sudden, surprising, unexpected things; but she loved them only if either she or God instigated them. Quite illogically she denied this privilege to others. She was distinctly irritated if anyone took her unawares either by a sudden gift or by an unexpected piece of news. She was so filled with life herself that she forever wanted to dispense rather than to receive, to initiate rather than to be initiated.

She loved sudden changes of weather, blizzards, line gales, the excitement of continuous winter cold, northern lights, falling stars; and during many years of her long and abundant life she had had her fill of such abrupt and whimsical behavior on the part of God. For she had spent much of her life at sea, where holidays were mere points in time, unprepared for, often even unnoticed, slipping upon one like all other days, recalled if wind and weather were kind, forgotten if God had other and more immediate means of attracting one's attention to His power and His might. She had spent Christmas in all kinds of strange places: off Cape Horn in a gale; running before the trades somewhere a thousand miles off Africa; in a typhoon off the Chinese coast; in the doldrums, where the twenty fifth of December was but twenty-four still hours in a succession of motionless days; in the bitter cold of a winter storm too near the treacherous cliffs of southern Ireland for comfort or security. Small wonder that she would find it difficult, after her half-reluctant return to village life, to tie up Christmas in a neat parcel and to label it with a date.

As children we were forever asking our grandmother about those Christmases at sea.

"Didn't you give any presents at all, Grandmother? Not to the sailors or even to Grandfather?"

"The sailors," said my grandmother, "had a tot of rum all around in the dogwatch if the weather was fair. That was the sailors' present."

We always smile over "tot." This facetious, trifling word attached to one of such enormity as "rum" in those days of temperance agitation seemed impious to say the least. "What is a tot of rum, Grandmother?"

"A tot," answered my grandmother with great dignity, "is an indeterminate quantity."

"Did the sailors sing Christmas carols when they had the tot?"

"They did not. They sang songs which no child should ever know."

"Then did you and Grandfather have no presents at all, Grandmother?"

"Whenever we got to port we had our presents; that is, if we did not forget that we had had no Christmas. We had Christmas in January or even March. Christmas, children, is not a date. It is a state of mind."

Christmas to my grandmother was always a state of mind. Once she had left the sea, once she was securely on land, where the behavior of God was less exciting, she began to supplement Providence and Fate by engendering excitement in those about her. Her objection to Christmas lay in the fact that it was a day of expectation, when no one could possibly be taken by surprise. She endured it with forbearance, but she disliked it heartily.

Unlike most women of her generation, she cared not a whit for tradition or convention; but she remained to the end of her days the unwilling prey of both. Unlike most women of any generation, she scorned possessions, and she saw to it that she suffered them briefly. We knew from the beginning the fate of the gifts we annually bestowed upon her; yet we followed the admonition and example of our parents in bestowing them. From our scanty Christmas allowance of two dollars each with which to purchase presents for a family of ten, we set aside a generous portion for Grandmother's gift. She was always with us at Christmas and received our offerings without evident annoyance, knowing that what she must endure for a brief season she could triumph over in the days to come.

As we grew older and were allowed at length to select our gifts free from parental supervision, we began to face the situation precisely as it was. Instead of black silk gloves for Grandmother, we chose for her our own favorite perfumery; we substituted plain white handkerchiefs for the black-edged ones which she normally carried; a box of chocolates took the place of one of peppermints; a book called *Daily Thoughts for Daily Needs* was discarded in favor of a story by Anna Katharine Green.

My grandmother waited for a fortnight or longer after Christmas before she proffered her gifts to family, neighbors, and friends. By early January, she concluded, expectation would have vanished and satiety be forgotten; in other words, the first fine careless rapture of sudden surprise and pleasure might again be abroad in the world. She invariably chose a dull or dark day upon which to deliver her presents. Around three o'clock on some dreary afternoon was her time for setting forth. Over her coat she tied one of her stout aprons of black sateen, and in its capacious lap she cast all her own unwanted gifts—a black silk umbrella, odd bits of silver and jewelry, gloves, handkerchiefs, stockings, books, candies, Florida water, underwear, bedroom slippers, perfumeries, knickknacks of every sort; even family photographs were not excluded! Thus she started upon her rounds, returning at supper-time empty-handed and radiant.

I remember how once as children we met her thus burdened on our way home from school.

"You're rather late for Christmas, Grandmother," we ventured together.

"So, my dears, were the Three Wise Men!" she said.

The many days foretold by the preacher for the return of bread thus cast upon the waters have in the case of my grandmother not yet elapsed. For, although she has long since gone where possessions are of no account, and where, for all we know, life is a succession of quick surprises, I receive from time to time the actual return of her Christmas gifts so freely and curiously dispensed. Only last Christmas a package revealed a silver pie knife marked with her initials, and presented to her, I remembered with a start, through the combined sacrificial resources of our entire family fully thirty years before. An accompanying note bore these words:

> Your grandmother brought this knife to my mother twenty-eight years ago as a Christmas gift. I remember how she came one rainy afternoon in January with the present in her apron. I found it recently among certain of my mother's things, and knowing your grandmother's strange ways as to Christmas gifts, I feel that honesty demands its return to you. You may be interested in this card which accompanied it.

Tied to the silver pie knife by a bit of red ribbon obviously salvaged long ago from Christmas plenty was a card inscribed on both sides. On one side was written: "To grandmother with Christmas love from her children and grandchildren" and on the other: "To my dear friend, Lizzie Osgood, with daily love from Eliza Ann Chase."

# Go Tell It on the Mountain

JOHN W. WORK JR.

SPIRITUAL

Go, tell it on the moun - tain, o - ver the hills and ev-'ry-where;

*Fine*

Go, tell it on the moun - tain, that Je - sus Christ is born.

1. While shep - herds kept their watch - ing o'er
2. The shep - herds feared and trem - bled when,
3. Down in a low - ly man - ger the

si - lent flocks by night, be - hold, thro' - out the
lo! a - bove the earth rang out the an - gel
hum - ble Christ was born, and God sent us sal -

*D.C.*

heav - ens there shone a ho - ly light.
cho - rus that hailed our Sav - iour's birth.
va - tion that bless - ed Christ - mas morn.

## Bethlehem of Judea

Author Unknown

A little child,
A shining star.
A stable rude,
The door ajar.

Yet in that place,
So crude, forlorn,
The Hope of all
The world was born.

## May These Be Your Gifts

Author Unknown

May these be your gifts at Christmas—
Warm hearts and shining faces,
Surrounding you to make your home
The happiest of places.

May these be your gifts at Christmas—
Deep peace and lasting love,
That you will share together
With the ones you're fondest of.

May these be your gifts at Christmas—
The promise of a year
Where everything goes well with you
And those you hold most dear.

## A Christmas Hymn

Christina G. Rossetti

Love came down at Christmas,
Love all lovely, Love Divine;
Love was born at Christmas,
Star and Angels gave the sign.

Love shall be our token,
Love be yours and love be mine,
Love to God and all men,
Love for plea and gift and sign.

## There's More to Christmas

Author Unknown

There's more, much more, to Christmas
Than candlelight and cheer;
It's the spirit of sweet friendship
That brightens all the year;
It's thoughtfulness and kindness,
It's hope reborn again,
For peace, for understanding
And for goodwill to men!

*May you have the greatest two gifts of
all on these holidays: Someone to love
and someone who loves you.*   —*John Sinor*

# THE THREE WISE MEN OF TOTENLEBEN

Alexander Lernet-Holenia
Translated by Judith Bernays Heller

*I*n November of the year 1647, the commander-in-chief of the French forces during the Thirty Years War, Marshal Turenne, set out on a long journey. His horsemen picked up two young people who were traveling through the country, poorly clad and on foot. One was a young man, the other a young woman. The woman was pregnant, perhaps already in her seventh or eighth month. Questioned, they replied they were husband and wife, who had been forced to leave the place where they had been living with the wife's parents. They were now on their way to the husband's home—a village called Totenleben on the lower Main River, where they hoped to find living quarters and perhaps some means of livelihood as well.

Marshal Turenne took in only snatches of this. Nevertheless he noted the odd name of the village which was the goal of the young people. He dismissed them, and then reached a decision.

One night he suddenly appeared in the region of the lower Main. Both he and his men were armed and wrapped in warm coats and furs. The moon glistened on their helmets. All the land around was devastated. Preceding the troop by some hundred paces, two horsemen with rifles in their hands stopped now and again in front of a clump of snow-covered bushes or at the ruins of a burned

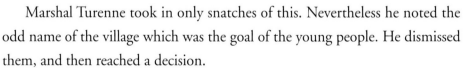

farm and cried out: "Who goes there?" But there was no one to answer. The whole region lay still as in death. As the cavalcade pressed steadily forward, silver hoarfrost spun its web in the icy ruts.

The riders stopped at the edge of a wood. Turenne dismounted and two henchmen apparently according to orders previously given, approached him and removed his fur coat and hat. The moonlight gleamed on the gold chain he wore around his neck.

Meanwhile, several of his officers had gotten off their horses and approached him while the serving men pulled a garment over his armor. It was a white robe, bespangled with golden stars. They covered his face with a black veil. The whole was the costume for the eve of Twelfth Night, such as waits or carol singers wear. The servants took the pistols from his saddlebag and placed them in his hands.

"I am going now," he said to his officers. "Wait for me here. If I have not returned by three o'clock in the morning, then have the village search for me."

"Yes, your excellency," was the officers' reply. The Marshal departed alone, trudging over the field of snow.

He had walked several hundred paces when the silhouette of a village appeared before him. At its northern boundary a light was shining. Toward this he made his way. The beam came from a peculiar lantern made out of oiled paper in the shape of a star and attached to a pole some eight feet high.

Two men, one of whom carried the pole, stood by the light. They too wore the costume of waits, though the veils they wore were white.

Turenne raised his pistols and stepped up to them as he gave his own name. The two answered, giving their names: "Wrangel," and "Melander." They were, respectively, the commander-in-chief of the Swedes, newly appointed after Torstenson's retirement, and the Supreme Chief of the Imperial Armies, Count Melander of Holzapfel.

All three of them now raised their veils and looked into one another's eyes, then let the veils fall once more over their faces. Turenne hid his pistols under his robe, and said: "I have asked you gentlemen to come here in this disguise so that we may be able to discuss the matters that concern us, undisturbed and in secret. This is the eve of Twelfth Night and we shall be taken for waits. We would do best to proceed to the village to find quarters."

"There is no longer any village," said Melander. "It has been burned to the ground. Your own troops, Count, may have set fire to it."

"Be that as it may," said Wrangel, "we ought to see to it that we find some shelter somewhere. Surely we do not want to stand about here in the cold."

Accordingly they began to move on with their star. Along the village street there were only heaps of rubble where once there had been houses. But near the burned-out church they managed to find a house passably preserved, with its windows boarded up. A faint light shone from between the boards.

They went up to the door and knocked. They had to do this repeatedly before a voice from within inquired what they wanted.

"Open the door," they called, whereupon the door, which no longer had any hinges, was pulled back a bit with a creak. A man stuck his head out.

"What's your business?" he asked.

"We are waits," said Melander. "Let us in."

"Waits?" the man asked. "So early?"

"Yes," said Melander. "Let us in." He crossed the threshold, followed by the two others, after they had put aside the pole with the lantern.

"But look here," said the man, after closing the door behind them, "today is only Christmas Eve."

"No, indeed," said Wrangel, "it's Twelfth Night. Do you people here still go by the old calendar?

The pope has changed the calendar," said Melander. "It was already fourteen days behind, and no longer agreed with the position of the stars. Don't you know that?"

"The village is in ruins," said the man. "The whole countryside is desolate. How should we know whether the pope has changed the calendar or not? We are celebrating Christmas Eve today, if you can still call it celebrating."

"Well," said Wrangel, "never mind. We would like to stay for awhile. Bring us something to eat. We'll pay you in good honest coin."

"I used to be the innkeeper here," said the man, "and my business prospered. But now I have scarcely bread enough for my own family, and if we are thirsty, we have to drink melted snow, for our wells are all stopped up. Sit down, for a seat is all I have to offer. What manner of men are you to believe that you can get alms by singing as waits? Where do you come from? Here, in this village, we are the only ones left alive; and there is not a grain of wheat or a single beast left in the whole region. Everything has been destroyed by the war."

The three commanders looked about them. All they saw was a hearth on which a fire cast its flickering light and a table with a few benches. Smoke filled the room. The innkeeper's wife and a half-grown boy were watching the strangers. In addition, there were two other people in the room—a young man and his young wife. Turenne recognized them as the same two whom he had encountered on his reconnaissance trip.

"Who are they?" he asked in faulty German.

"They are poor people," said the innkeeper, "who came to this place but who could find no shelter anywhere. The man was originally from here; he moved away and got married. But he had to come back, and now I've given them a lodging in the stable. The wife is expecting a child."

"You don't say!" said Turenne. The three strangers sat down at the table.

In the meantime, the others busied themselves near the hearth setting up a Christmas crèche of moss and small wooden figures. They were brightly colored and represented the Holy Family, the angels, the adoring Magi, the shepherds, the ox and the ass. For a while the three generals looked on; then they began their talk. They spoke in French.

"The peace talks that started last year," said Turenne, "are not being conducted in the interest of the armies. If peace were to come, there would be no need to have armed forces. To discuss together what measures should be taken against the conclusion of an overhasty peace is the purpose of my invitation. For even though we are enemies, we are all in the same boat; however you look at it, what's good for one is good for all three of us."

When those who were setting up the crèche heard the talk in a foreign language, they looked over at the three in surprise. For a time the innkeeper listened anxiously, then he approached the table.

"Who are you?" he asked. "You are no ordinary waits. You are foreigners and perhaps soldiers as well. Haven't you convinced yourself hat this country, this village, this house are in ruins and that there's nothing more for you to carry off? What do you want from us? Have you been sent by those who want to take our very lives? That is the only thing you can still take from us."

"Be still," said Melander, "we are the Three Wise Men. We have to discuss something here." And he threw him a golden coin.

The innkeeper looked at the gold piece, for he had not seen its like for many a year. He took it quickly and tested it with his fingers. At the same time, his bearing changed. He wanted to look into the faces of the three, yet his glance could not penetrate their veils. Only now did he notice the boots and spurs visible below their robes, and the metal ends of their leather sword sheaths.

"Your pardon, my lords!" he said, bowing obsequiously, "I would not for the world . . . I did not know . . ."

"Very well, very well," said Melander, "leave us alone."

"May we at least," said the innkeeper, "sing the Christmas song for the gentlemen? It will not disturb you?"

"Sing it, for all I care," said Melander, "but do it quietly."

After some time, those around the crèche began to sing the Christmas song. Toward the end of the song, the young wife stopped singing; she tottered, and clung to her husband. Her pains had begun.

Had it not been for the strangers, the innkeeper would have allowed her to remain in the room and have her baby there. But in the presence of the others he did not dare to do this. The woman was led into the stable where she lay on a pile of moss and dead leaves.

The generals had not noticed when the woman was led out the room. Suddenly the generals appeared to be at odds now, and their voices rose in excitement. It was Melander who pronounced himself most emphatically as against continuation of the war. He said that surely the country was sufficiently desolate, it was plain to see how poverty-stricken the people had become here as

well as elsewhere. And so the three went on quarreling until a cry and then another was heard coming from the stable. They looked up.

"What's the matter?" asked Wrangel, but now all was quiet. "Who screamed out there?" asked Wrangel. "What is going on out there?"

"Oh, sir!" said the innkeeper.

"What is it?" Wrangel cried. "What's the matter?"

"Just imagine, sire," said the innkeeper, "the young wife gave birth to a child, a boy. Perhaps, after all, peace will come soon."

The three looked at one another. For a long time they had not heard anyone speak in tones such as the innkeeper used. The child was the child of strangers, it was no concern of his, and yet he was as moved as if it had indeed been his own. For here, in this destroyed countryside, resembling an icy waste covered with the corpses of the dead, a child had begun to live—breathing a breath of spring. In the midst of the triumph of death, which was the daily business of the generals, a child had been born, and it seemed as if it had been born also unto them.

The first to step through the threshold of the stable door was Melander. He was followed by Wrangel, and then Turenne. There lay the woman on her bed of straw. The others knelt around her as they wrapped the baby in a few odds and ends of old rags and laid the child in her arms.

The generals stood there in silence and gazed upon the mother and child for a long time. Then Turenne removed the golden chain which he wore under his Twelfth Night robe and placed it near the child. Melander pulled off his glove and took a ruby ring from his finger, and Wrangel laid a pouch full of money down on the bed of straw.

To those who received the gifts, it seemed as if a miracle had happened. The young man wanted to express his faltering thanks but was not able to utter a single word. They soon departed, leaving behind them their strange lantern, and ordered the innkeeper, who was chattering and laughing and who continued to wipe his eyes, to stay behind when he wanted to accompany them.

At the outskirts of the village, they saluted one another curtly, and each one went on his way, their talk unfinished.

But in their hearts was peace.

Gifts *from the* Heart

# THE ART OF GIVING

Gerald Horton Bath

One of my favorite stories is about a missionary teaching in Africa. Before Christmas, he had been telling his African students how Christians, as an expression of their joy, gave each other presents on Christ's birthday.

On Christmas morning one of the Africans brought the missionary a seashell of lustrous beauty. When asked where he had discovered such an extraordinary shell, the young man said he had walked many miles to a certain bay, the only spot where such shells could be found.

"I think it was wonderful of you to travel so far to get this lovely gift for me," the teacher exclaimed.

His eyes brightening, the African answered, "Long walk, part of gift."

> *A gift, however small, speaks its own language. And when it tells of the love of the giver, it is truly blessed.*
> —*Norman Vincent Peale*

# CHRISTMAS IS IN THE UNEXPECTED

Faith Baldwin

Christmas is in the unexpected gift: flowers from an acquaintance; a telephone call from someone you haven't heard from in years, and who, you thought, had forgotten you; it is in a card from overseas, a letter from a stranger, and a clumsily wrapped, handmade atrocity, fashioned by a child who has labored long, and with sticky hands.

None of this is basically material.

Christmas is an urge to give, to do, to be. It may last a very short time— and usually does—but, during it, the human spirit attains a fractional growth.

# A Gift from the Heart

Norman Vincent Peale

ew York City, where I live, is impressive at any time, but as Christmas approaches, it's overwhelming. Store windows blaze— with light and color, furs and jewels. Golden angels, forty feet tall, hover over Fifth Avenue. Wealth, power, opulence . . . nothing in the world can match this fabulous display.

Through the gleaming canyons, people hurry to find last-minute gifts. Money seems to be no problem. If there's a problem, it's that the recipients so often have everything they need or want that it's hard to find anything suitable, anything that will really say "I love you."

Last December, as Christ's birthday drew near, a stranger was faced with just that problem. She had come from Switzerland to live in an American home and perfect her English. In return, she was willing to act as secretary, mind the grandchildren, do anything she was asked. She was just a girl in her late teens. Her name was Ursula.

One of the tasks her employers gave Ursula was keeping track of Christmas presents as they arrived. There were many, and all would require an acknowledgement. Ursula kept a faithful record but with a growing sense of concern. She was grateful to her American friends; she wanted to show her gratitude by giving them a Christmas present. But nothing that she could buy with her small allowance could compare with the gifts she was recording daily. Besides, even without these gifts, it seemed to her that her employer already had everything.

At night, from her window, Ursula could see the snowy expanse of Central Park and beyond it the jagged skyline of the city. Far below, in the restless streets, taxis hooted and traffic lights winked red and green. It was so different from the silent majesty of the Alps that at times she had to blink back tears of the homesickness she was careful never to show. It was in the solitude of her little room, a few days before Christmas, that her secret idea came to Ursula.

It was almost as if a voice spoke clearly, inside her head. "It's true," said the voice, "that many people in this city have much more than you do. But surely there are many people who have far less. If thou will think about this, you may find a solution to what's troubling you."

Ursula thought long and hard. Finally on her day off, which was Christmas Eve, she went to a great department store. She moved slowly along the crowded aisles, selecting and rejecting things in her mind. At last she bought something, and had it wrapped in gaily colored paper. She went out into the gray twilight and looked helplessly around. Finally she went up to a doorman, resplendent in blue and gold. "Excuse, please," she said in her hesitant English, "can you tell me where to find a poor street?"

"A poor street, miss?" said the puzzled man.

"Yes, a very poor street. The poorest in the city."

The doorman looked doubtful. "Well, you might try Harlem. Or down in the Village. Or the Lower East Side, maybe."

But these names meant nothing to Ursula. She thanked the doorman and walked along, threading her way through the stream of shoppers until she came to a tall policeman. "Please," she said, "can you direct me to a very poor street in . . . in Harlem?"

The policeman looked at her sharply and shook his head. "Harlem's no place for you, miss." And he blew his whistle and sent the traffic swirling past.

Holding her package carefully, Ursula walked on, head bowed against the sharp wind. If a street looked poorer than the one she was on, she took it. But none seemed like the slums she had heard about. Once she stopped a woman, "Please, where do the very poor people live?" But the woman gave her a stare and hurried on.

Darkness came sifting from the sky, Ursula was cold and discouraged and afraid of becoming lost. She came to an intersection and stood forlornly on the corner. What she was trying to do suddenly seemed foolish, impulsive, absurd. Then, through the traffic's roar, she heard the cheerful tinkle of a bell. On the corner opposite, a Salvation Army man was making his traditional Christmas appeal.

At once Ursula felt better; the Salvation Army was a part of life in Switzerland, too. Surely this man could tell her what she wanted to know. She waited for the light, then crossed over to him. "Can you help me? I'm looking for a baby. I have here a little present for the poorest baby I can find." And she held up the package with the green ribbon and the gaily colored paper.

Dressed in gloves and overcoat a size too big for him, he seemed a very ordinary man. But behind his steel-rimmed glasses his eyes were kind. He looked at Ursula and stopped ringing his bell. "What sort of present?" he asked.

"A little dress. For a small, poor baby. Do you know of one?"

"Oh, yes," he said. "'Of more than one, I'm afraid."

"Is it far away? I could take a taxi, maybe?"

The Salvation Army man wrinkled his forehead. Finally he said, "It's almost six o'clock. My relief will show up then. If you want to wait, and if you afford a dollar taxi ride, I'll take you to a family in my neighborhood who needs just about everything."

"And they have a small baby?"

"A very small baby."

"Then," said Ursula joyfully, "I wait!"

The substitute bell-ringer came. A cruising taxi slowed. In its welcome warmth, she told her new friend about herself, how she came to be in New York, what she was trying to do. He listened in silence, and the taxi driver listened too. When they reached their destination, the driver said, "Take your time, missy, I'll wait for you."

On the sidewalk, Ursula stared up at the forbidding tenement—dark, decaying, saturated with hopelessness. A gust of wind, iron-cold, stirred the refuse in the street and rattled the reeling trash cans. "They live on the third floor," the Salvation Army man said. "Shall we go up?"

But Ursula shook her head. "They would try to thank me, and this is not from me." She pressed the package into his hand. "Take it up for me, please. Say it's from . . . from someone who has everything."

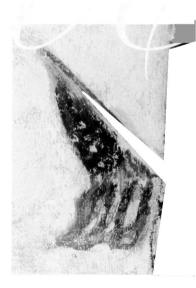

The taxi bore her swiftly from dark streets to lighted ones, from misery to abundance. She tried to visualize the Salvation Army man climbing the stairs, the knock, the explanation, the package being opened, the dress on the baby. It was hard to do.

Arriving at the apartment house on Fifth Avenue where she lived, she fumbled in her purse. But the driver flicked the flag up. "No charge, miss."

"No charge?" echoed Ursula, bewildered.

"Don't worry," the driver said. "I've been paid." He smiled at her and drove away.

Ursula was up early the next day. She set the table with special care. By the time she had finished, the family was awake, and there was all the excitement and laughter of Christmas morning. Soon the living room was a sea of gay discarded wrappings. Ursula thanked everyone for the presents she received. Finally when there was a lull, she began to explain hesitantly why there seemed to be none from her. She told about going to the department store. She told about the Salvation Army man. She told about the taxi driver. When she finished, there was a long silence. No one seemed to trust himself to speak. "So you see," said Ursula, "I try to do a kindness in your name. And this is my Christmas present to you."

How do I happen to know all this? I know it because ours was the home where Ursula lived. Ours was the Christmas she shared. We were like many Americans, so richly blessed that to this child from across the sea there seemed to be nothing she could add to the material things we already had. And so she offered something of far greater value: a gift from the heart, an act of kindness carried out in our name.

Strange, isn't it? A shy Swiss girl, alone in a great impersonal city. You would think that nothing she could do would affect anyone. And yet, by trying to give away love, she brought the true spirit of Christmas into our lives, the spirit of selfless giving. That was Ursula's secret—and she shared it with us all.

## The Heart Goes Home
Grace V. Watkins

Always the heart goes home on Christmas Eve,
Goes silently across a continent,
Or mountains, or the seas. A heart will leave
The glitter of a city street and, sent
By something deep and timeless, find the way
To a little cottage on a country hill.
And even if the little cottage may
Have disappeared, a heart will find it still.

The smile of tenderness upon the faces,
The simple words, the arms secure and strong,
The sweetness of the well-remembered places;
All these a heart will find and will belong
Once more to country hills, however far,
And sense the holy presence of the Star.

## *Lord of All*

Robert Herrick

The darling of the world is come,
And fit it is, we find a room
To welcome Him, to welcome Him.
The nobler part of all the house here
     is the heart,
Which we will give Him;
And bequeath this holly
     and this ivy wreath
To do Him honour; who's our King,
And Lord of all this revelling.

## *Hearts Go Home*

Alice Kennelly Roberts

The heart remembers Christmas and days of long ago,
When festive preparations made all the house aglow;
The kitchen fairly bubbled with turkey, puddings, pies,
And all those extra goodies which came as a surprise.

Each person had his duties, and old and young could share,
The little ones, and Grandma, and even Spot was there;
The fruitcake and the mincemeat, the chestnut dressing too;
The oranges and red apples filled childhood's world anew.

Yes, hearts go home at Christmas to take again their place,
To see at Christmas dinner each dear remembered face;
And though the scene we cherish is no longer there,
The love, the joys, the laughter are with us everywhere.

*When Christmastime makes its approach, my heart is homeward bound.* —Virginia Blanck Moore

# Joy to the World

Isaac Watts

George F. Handel

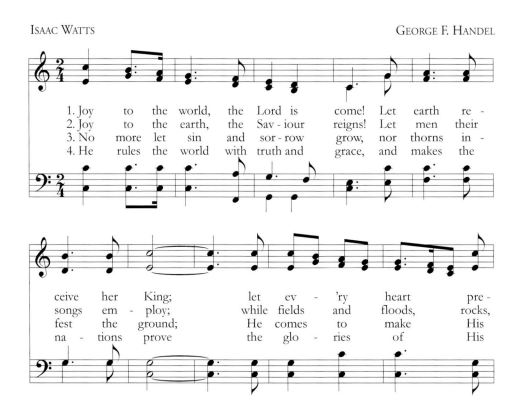

1. Joy to the world, the Lord is come! Let earth re-
2. Joy to the earth, the Sav - iour reigns! Let men their
3. No more let sin and sor - row grow, nor thorns in -
4. He rules the world with truth and grace, and makes the

ceive her King; let ev - 'ry heart pre-
songs em - ploy; while fields and floods, rocks,
fest the ground; He comes to make His
na - tions prove the glo - ries of His

women from many different countries. They too were away from home and familiar faces. We felt especially drawn to two students from Nigeria—Sam and his beautiful cousin Iba. In the days following the party we saw quite a lot of them and got to know them very well. And then, one day when the question, "What shall we do at Christmas?" came up, the answer was obvious. Invite Sam and Iba to spend the day with us! Just because we weren't back home in the familiar surroundings, keeping the old traditions, sharing the day with our family-family, that didn't mean we had to be alone. Right outside our door there was another family that extended throughout the whole world . . . there were people who needed to be included in our lives just as much as we needed to have them with us. Sam and Iba—and any of their friends who didn't have a place to go on Christmas day—they were our heart-family!

On the other three Christmases we had spent as a married couple, my parents were the ones who did everything for me. They prepared the dinner and opened their house to us . . . and during all the other earlier years of my life I had been poured into by those who loved and cared for me. . . . I had been the child receiving, but now it was different . . . I was the woman whose privilege it was to provide, to prepare. I loved the feeling of it!

And prepare I did. I wanted to blend as many of our cultural traditions into the newness of our situation as I possibly could. We had a tree—a small one—decorated with a few ornaments I bought at the five-and-ten. Louie supplied the wood for our fireplace and we had a crackling fire burning all day, which thoroughly delighted our little son. I tried to collect the ingredients for a typical American Christmas dinner, but since some items were scarce (the war was not long over) I had to improvise. For instance, I couldn't get sweet potatoes, so I cooked carrots in large chunks and baked them with brown sugar.

We spent Christmas day in 1953 with our heart-family—Sam and Iba and a room full of other students who came in their colorful native dress. It was a wonderful day, one I shall never forget. We read the Christmas story from Matthew and Luke and we sang carols and laughed and embraced and shared the deep joy we felt in the knowledge that we were children of God. The Nigerians were such lively, animated people who spoke so openly of their love for Christ . . . and it was this love which bound us together, making us truly brothers and sisters of one another. And then I understood what Jesus meant when he said, "Who is my brother and my sister? These people are, those who do the will of God." Sam and Iba and their wonderful friends were our friends now . . . they were new to my life . . . they were not part of my past . . . they were not the familiar faces I had longed to see at Christmas—but they were part of my present and part of my future. And they were our family!

Because we were unable to keep our traditional Christmas that year, we spent it in untraditional ways . . . and we discovered that it is more important to keep the spirit of Christmas than to keep the customs with which we have grown up. Yes, we still love the traditions and keep them whenever we can, and we love to be with our family-family whenever we can . . . but we are grateful for the times when this was not possible, for the times when we couldn't be with our relatives and friends—and yet Christmas still happened . . . and in a most spirit-warming way.

Sometimes life doesn't come to us; sometimes we have to reach out for it. People won't always come to us and instead of sitting home, waiting for someone to arrive, succumbing to the loneliness that comes to all of us when we are not with those who care for us, we have to reach out to those we need. Instead of asking ourselves, "Who's going to invite me for dinner?" why not ask, "Whom can I cook dinner for?"

After we returned from Scotland we began to form our own Christmas traditions as a family. Instead of going to my parents, we had them with us in our home, first in Bel Air and then in La Jolla, California, where Louie was called to serve two wonderful churches. As our children grew up they looked forward to these special gatherings each year. There were six of us now in our nuclear family—Louie and I, and our four children, Dan, Tim, Andie, and Jim—and at Christmastime our house was filled with friends as well as relatives and that was the only place in the world where we wanted to be on that day.

A few years ago my husband received a call to National Presbyterian Church in Washington, D.C., and we knew that that year would be our last in La Jolla. Our family gathering would be especially dear to us, for we would carry its memories for a long, long time.

And then we learned that my parents—Grandma and Grandpa Wilhelm—would not be with us. Grandpa had to undergo surgery and would have to spend Christmas day in a hospital north of Los Angeles. So we mailed our gifts to each other and bit our lips a little in our disappointment.

If it had been just Louie and I at Christmas, I would have suggested driving up to Los Angeles and spending the day with Grandpa, but I just couldn't ask our children to do that. The trip took three-and-a-half hours each way, which meant that we would have to be away from home all day, and our sons and daughter so enjoyed being home at Christmas. I knew their friends would be dropping in all day—and that soon our children would be saying good-bye to these friends for at least a long time. So I put the idea out of my mind.

On Christmas morning we did what we always did as a family. We got up very early, had a light breakfast and then we sat around the tree while one of us read the Christmas story from the Gospels. Then we opened our presents, hugging and kissing each other for the thoughtfulness and remembered wishes we found wrapped up in the packages. But it wasn't the same without Grandma and Grandpa. We missed them very much. Our

tall, long-haired boys were touchingly open about their feelings. "I sure miss Grandpa." "He's so much fun!" "Yea, he's a real cruiser!" and Andie's sensitive face and the sadness in her large compassionate eyes said more than words.

It was time for me to take the turkey out of the refrigerator and put it in the oven, and I was glad to have an excuse to go into the kitchen because I thought I was going to cry a little. And I honestly don't know which one of our children said it first, but somebody said, "Hey, how would the rest of you

feel about driving up to Los Angeles and seeing Grandma and Grandpa?"

Before I reached the kitchen the others agreed.

"Yeah, that's what I'd like to do!"

"Let's drive up and see them."

"It's not the same without them."

The turkey never got out of the refrigerator that Christmas day. We left it, stuffed and ready, for another time. We piled into the car. We took along our

projector and a few slides from our summer backpacking trip so that we could show them to my parents.

It was a long drive to the hospital and when we got there the corridors were almost empty. Doctors had sent home as many patients as they could, because everyone knows that a hospital is no place to spend the holidays. We found Grandpa's room and looked in. There he was, sitting up in bed, with Grandma in a straight-backed chair by his bedside. When Grandpa saw us, the tears began to roll down his cheeks and he cried like a little boy over-whelmed with a joy that is just too big for him to hold inside himself. He couldn't get over the fact that we—and especially the children—would choose to drive so far to be with him on this day, this year.

We had a wonderful visit and Grandpa kept saying, "This is the best Christmas I've ever had." We talked and laughed and showed our slides on the white hospital walls and reminisced about our summer vacation in the Sierras. We stayed for several hours, and before we left we all joined hands around Grandpa's bed and thanked God for this day when we were able to be together with our loved ones.

When we left Grandpa's room, we were hungry so we went downstairs to the hospital cafeteria which was about to close. There was very little food left—some cole slaw, some dishes of gelatin with whipped cream, and a few cartons of milk—and that was our Christmas dinner. I'm sure that everyone felt as I did, that it was one of the richest Christmases we'd ever had.

On the way home we were cozy and close in our car and so filled with the spirit of Christmas. Once again life had shown us that traditions, lovely as they are, do not make Christmas. Christmas happens wherever we are—at home, in another land, among friends and family, among strangers, in a hospital room, on the road to somewhere—in the midst of the familiar or on the threshold of the new and unexpected—as long as our hearts are open to the love that Christ brought us when Christmas happened that first time.

# A Prayer at Christmas

Author Unknown

Give us the faith of innocent children, that we may look forward with hope in our hearts to the dawn of happy tomorrows. Reawaken the thought that our most cherished desires will be realized—the things closest to our hearts—that we may come to an appreciation of the limitless joys and bountiful rewards of Patience, Charity, and Sacrifice.

Above all, endow us with the spirit of courage, that we may face the perplexities of a troubled world without flinching, imbued with the child-like faith which envisions the beautiful and inspiring things of life, and restore the happy hours and experiences so many of us foolishly believe are lost forever.

Give us faith in ourselves and faith in our fellow man, then the treasures and beauties of life that make man happy will spring from an inexhaustible source.

And at Christmas, when the hearts of the world swell in joyous celebration, let us cast aside the pretense of sturdy men and live, if only for a day, in the hope and joy we knew as children.

# A Prayer for Christmas Morning

Henry Van Dyke

The day of joy returns, Father in Heaven, and crowns another year with peace and good will. Help us rightly to remember the birth of Jesus, that we may share in the song of the angels, the gladness of the shepherds, and the worship of the wise men. Close the doors of hate and open the doors of love all over the world. . . . Let kindness come with every gift and good desires with every greeting. Deliver us from evil, by the blessing that Christ brings, and teach us to be merry with clean hearts. May the Christmas morning make us happy to be thy children, and the Christmas evening bring us to our bed with grateful thoughts, forgiving and forgiven, for Jesus' sake. Amen.

# THE YEAR THE PRESENTS DIDN'T COME

Ben Logan

*C*atalogs, it must be understood, were our department stores. Visitors from a marvelous place somewhere outside our world, they said Christmas was coming, that once a year a spirit of extravagance brought us a select few of all the wonderful things on display.

The catalog orders would go into the mail and our choices began to grow, becoming our own creations. Every morning when I first woke up, I would stay under the covers a moment, shut my eyes tight and try to see what was happening. After five days, I decided the letter had arrived in Chicago. Two more days—no, make it three because they were busy—to find our things and ship them. Then another five days for the packages to come. I added one more day because that made it Saturday and I could run to meet the mailman myself. Mr. Holliday was driving a sled by then because there was too much snow for his Model T. He poked through the packages in the sled box. "Sorry," he said. "Not here yet."

The days crept by. Each afternoon we waited in the cold for Mr. Holliday. He would search through the sled for the packages he already knew were not there and say, "Maybe tomorrow."

On the day before Christmas, we raced to the mailbox with a pail of steaming coffee for Mr. Holliday. "You know," he said, not looking at us, "I guess nothing came, but I'll just look one more time." He sorted through the packages. We knew there wasn't anything there for us. He was just trying to make us feel better, or maybe make himself feel better.

We stayed there at the mailbox looking at each other. We didn't believe it. I was crying when we went to the house. Mother held me. "We'll still have Christmas, you know."

"Without our presents?"

Something changed in her face. "There's more to Christmas than presents."

When we carried the tree in and set it up in the dining room, the fresh snow began to melt into hundreds of shiny beads of water.

"Look!" Mother said. "It's already decorated."

We popped corn and made strings, the white corn alternating with the

cranberries. We got out all the old ornaments, handing to Father the star that went beyond our reach. The folded paper ornaments were opened to become bright-colored balls, stars, and bells. Mother began to hum a Christmas carol. It was just like all the other remembered afternoons leading up to Christmas Eve.

The house was very still when I woke on Christmas morning. Treelike patterns of frost covered the lower half of my window, turned red-gold by the beginning color on the eastern horizon. Far out across a white meadow I could see smoke rising from the chimney of a neighbor's house, reminding me that other people were having Christmas.

For each of us there was a basket filled with English walnuts, pecans, almonds, ribbon candy, peanut brittle, chocolate stars, and one bright navel orange and a big Red Delicious apple. I sorted through my basket, silenced by the strangeness of having no presents to open and the thought of an empty day stretching ahead.

Mother went to the kitchen to work on Christmas dinner. We four boys followed and worked with her. I don't think that had ever happened before. My new toys had always captured me on Christmas morning, pulling me away into a play world that did not include anyone else.

We made sugar cookies, eating them hot and buttery right from the oven almost as fast as we cut out new ones. The chickens were already cooking, filling the house with a rich roasting smell. Junior brought his guitar into the kitchen and we sang as we worked. Not Christmas carols. They were for later. Everyone kept talking about earlier Christmases, every other sentence beginning with "Remember the time . . ."

Everyone was busy every minute. There were hickory nuts to crack, bowls to lick, coffee to grind, cream to whip. We kept splitting more firewood and feeding the kitchen range to keep the fire just right.

Finally, we all helped carry the steaming dishes to the dining room table with its white tablecloth that was trimmed with lace. There was a solemn moment and then the food itself, delicious and unending.

After dinner, Father left the table and put on his heavy jacket. We knew what he was going to do. Every year he took down a sheaf of oats that had been hanging on the wall since harvest and carried it outside for the birds. This time we put on our coats and went with him.

"It was something we did in Norway," he told us. "But there it would always be wheat."

He hung the oats on the big maple tree and we stepped back and waited, standing very still. A blue jay swooped in and peered at the grain. A bright red cardinal came and began to eat. Then a whole flock of English sparrows arrived, noisy and quarrelsome, reminding me of the four of us.

We cleared the snow away, brought kindling and sticks of oak from the woodshed and soon had a roaring bonfire in the yard. I ran to tell Mother, and she put on her coat and joined us.

Even then I don't think I realized how different the day had been. That is the way of Christmas stories. Their meanings have to grow with the seasons and the telling, and we only remember what we have learned by keeping the past alive.

Gifts from On High

# THE SPIRIT OF GIVING

Kate Douglas Wiggin

When the Child of Nazareth was born, the sun, according to the Bosnian legend, "leaped in the heavens, and the stars around it danced. A peace came over mountain and forest. Even the rotten stump stood straight and healthy on the green hillside. The grass was beflowered with open blossoms, incense sweet as myrrh pervaded upland and forest, birds sang on the mountain top, and all gave thanks to the great God."

It is naught but an old folktale, but it has truth hidden at its heart, for a strange, subtle force, a spirit of genial goodwill, a newborn kindness, seem to animate child and man alike when the world pays its tribute to the "heaven-sent youngling," as the poet Drummond calls the infant Christ.

When the three wise men rode from the east into the west on that "first, best Christmas night," they bore on their saddlebows three caskets filled with gold and frankincense and myrrh to be laid at the feet of the manger-cradled babe of Bethlehem. Beginning with this old, old journey, the spirit of giving crept into the world's heart. As the Magi came bearing gifts, so do we also; gifts that relieve wants, gifts that are sweet and fragrant with friendship, gifts that breathe love, gifts that mean service, gifts inspired still by the star that shone over the city of David nearly two thousand years ago.

Then hang the green coronet of the Christmas-tree with glittering baubles and jewels of flame; heap offerings on its emerald branches; bring the Yule log to the firing; deck the house with holly and mistletoe,

And all the bells on earth shall ring
On Christmas day in the morning.

*Who can forget—never to be forgot—the time, that all the world in slumber lies, when, like the stars, the singing angels shot to earth, and heaven awaked all his eyes to see another sun at midnight rise.* —Giles Fletcher

## Christmas Carol

J. R. Newell

From the starry heaven's descending
Herald angels in their flight,
Nearer winging,
Clearer singing,
Thrilled with harmony the night:
"Glory, glory in the highest!"
Sounded yet and yet again,
Sweeter, clearer,
Fuller, nearer–
"Peace on earth, good will to men!"

Shepherds in the field abiding,
Roused from sleep, that gladsome morn,
Saw the glory,
Heard the story
That the Prince of Peace was born:
"Glory, glory in the highest!"
Sang the angel choir again,
Nearer winging,
Clearer singing:
"Peace on earth, good will to men!"

Swept the angel singers onward,
Died the song upon the air;
But the glory
Of that story
Grows and triumphs everywhere.
And when glow the Yuletide heavens,
Seems that glorious song again
Floating nearer,
Sweeter, clearer–
"Peace on earth, good will to men!"

## Rise up, Shepherd, and Follow

Author Unknown

There's a star in the East
On Christmas morn.
Rise up, shepherd, and follow!
It'll lead to the place
Where the Saviour's born.
Rise up, shepherd, and follow!
If you take good heed
To the angel's words and
Rise up, shepherd, and follow,
You'll forget your flocks,
You'll forget your herds.
Rise up, shepherd, and follow!
Leave your sheep, leave your lambs,
Rise up, shepherd, and follow!
Leave your ewes, leave your rams,
Rise up, shepherd, and follow!
Follow the Star of Bethlehem,
Rise up, shepherd, and follow!

*There's a song in the air!
There's a star in the sky!
There's a mother's deep
prayer and a baby's low
cry!* —Josiah Gilbert Holland

# CHRISTMAS ROSES

Alice Isabel Hazeltine

The sun had dropped below the western hills of Judea, and the stillness of night had covered the earth. The heavens were illumined only by numberless stars, which shone the brighter for the darkness of the sky. No sound was heard but the occasional howl of a jackal or the bleat of a lamb in the sheepfold. Inside a tent on the hillside slept the shepherd, Berachah, and his daughter, Madelon. The little girl lay restless—sleeping, waking, dreaming, until at last she roused herself and looked about her.

"Father," she whispered, "Oh, my father, awake. I fear for the sheep."

The shepherd turned himself and reached for his staff. "What hearest thou, daughter? The dogs are asleep. Hast thou been burdened by an evil dream?"

"Nay, but Father," she answered, "seest thou not the light? Hearest thou not the voice?"

Berachah gathered his mantle about him, rose, looked over the hills toward Bethlehem, and listened. The olive trees on yonder slope were casting their shadows in a marvellous light, unlike daybreak or sunset, or even the light of the moon. By the campfire below on the hillside the shepherds on watch were rousing themselves. Berachah waited and wondered, while Madelon clung to his side. Suddenly a sound rang out in the stillness. Madelon pressed still closer.

"It is the voice of an angel, my daughter. What it means I know not. Neither understand I this light." Berachah fell on his knees and prayed.

"Fear not: for, behold, I bring you good tidings of great joy, which shall be to all people. For unto you is born this day in the city of David a Saviour, which is Christ the Lord. And this shall be a sign unto you; Ye shall find the babe wrapped in swaddling clothes, lying in a manger."

The voice of the angel died away, and the air was filled with music. Berachah raised Madelon to her feet. "Ah, daughter," said he, "it is the wonder night so long expected. To us hath it been given to see the sign. It is the Messiah who hath come, the Messiah, whose name shall be called Wonderful, Counsellor, the mighty God, the Everlasting Father, the Prince of Peace. He it is who shall reign on the throne of David, He it is who shall redeem Israel."

Slowly up the hillside toiled the shepherds to the tent of Berachah, their chief, who rose to greet them eagerly.

"What think you of the wonder night and of the sign?" he queried. "Are we not above all others honored, to learn of the Messiah's coming?"

"Yea, and Berachah," replied their spokesman, Simon, "believest thou not that we should worship the infant King? Let us now go to Bethlehem and see this thing which has come to pass."

A murmur of protest came from the edge of the circle, and one or two turned impatiently away, whispering of duty toward flocks and the folly of searching for a new-born baby in the city of Bethlehem. Hardheaded, practical men were these, whose hearts had not been touched by vision or by song.

The others, however, turned expectantly toward Berachah, awaiting his decision. "Truly," said Jude, "the angel of the Lord hath given us the sign in order that we might go to worship Him. How can we then do otherwise? We shall find Him, as we have heard, lying in a manger. Let us not tarry, but let us gather our choicest treasures to lay at His feet and set out without delay across the hills toward Bethlehem."

"Oh, my Father," whispered Madelon, "permit me to go with thee." Berachah did not hear her but bade the men gather together their gifts.

"I, too, father?" asked Madelon. Still Berachah said nothing. Madelon slipped back into the tent, and throwing her arms around Melampo, her shepherd dog, whispered in his ear.

Soon the shepherds returned with their gifts. Simple treasures they were—a pair of cloves, a fine wool blanket, some eggs, some honey, some late autumn fruits. Berachah had searched for the finest of his flock—a snow-white lamb. Across the hills toward Bethlehem in the quiet, star-lit night they journeyed. As they moved silently along, the snow beneath their feet was changed to grass and flowers, and the icicles which had dropped from the trees covered their pathway like stars in the Milky Way.

Following at a distance, yet close enough to see them, came Madelon with Melampo at her heels. Over the hills they travelled on until Madelon lost sight of their own hillside. Farther and farther the shepherds went until they passed David's well and entered the city. Berachah led the way.

"How shall we know?" whispered Simon. And the others answered, "Hush, we must await the sign."

When at last they had compassed the crescent of Bethlehem's hills, they halted by an open doorway at a signal from their leader. "The manger," they joyfully murmured, "the manger! We have found the new-born King!"

One by one the shepherds entered. One by one they fell on their knees. Away in the shadow stood the little girl, her hand on Melampo's head. In wonder she gazed while the shepherds presented their gifts and were permitted each to hold for a moment the newborn Saviour. Melampo, the shepherd dog, crouched on the ground, as if he too, like the ox and the ass within, would worship the Child. Madelon turned toward the darkness weeping. Then, lifting her face to heaven, she prayed that God would bless Mother and Baby. Melampo moved closer to her, dumbly offering his companionship, and, raising his head, seemed to join in her petition. Once more she looked at the worshipping circle.

"Alas," she grieved, "no gift have I for the infant Saviour. Would that I had but a flower to place in His hand."

Suddenly Melampo stirred by her side, and as she turned again from the manger she saw before her an angel, the light from whose face illumined the darkness and whose look of tenderness rested on her tear-stained eyes.

"Why grievest thou, maiden?" asked the angel.

"That I come empty-handed to the cradle of the Saviour, that I bring no gift to greet Him," she murmured.

"The gift of thine heart, that is the best of all," answered the angel. "But that thou mayst carry something to the manger, see, I will strike with my staff upon the ground."

Wonderingly Madelon waited. From the dry earth wherever the angel's staff had touched sprang fair, white roses. Timidly she stretched out her hand toward the nearest ones. In the light of the angel's smile she gathered them, until her arms were filled with flowers. Again she turned toward the manger and quietly slipped to the circle of kneeling shepherds.

Closer she crept to the Child, longing, yet fearing, to offer her gift.

"How shall I know," she pondered, "whether He will receive this my gift as His own?

Berachah gazed in amazement at Madelon and the roses which she held. How came his child there, his child whom he had left safe on the hillside? And whence came such flowers? Truly this was a wonder night.

Step by step she neared the manger, knelt, and placed a rose in the Baby's hand. As the shepherds watched in silence, Mary bent over her Child, and Madelon waited for a sign. "Will He accept them?" she questioned. "How, oh, how shall I know?" As she prayed in humble silence, the Baby's eyes opened slowly, and over His face spread a smile.

# Christmas Still

Phillips Brooks

The silent skies are full of speech
For who hath ears to hear;
The winds are whispering each to each,
The moon is calling to the beech,
And stars their sacred mission teach,
Of Faith and Love and Fear.

But once the sky its silence broke
And song o'erflowed the earth,
The midnight air with glory shook,
And angels mortal language spoke
When God our human nature took
In Christ the Savior's birth.

And Christmas once is Christmas still;
The gates through which He came,
And forests wild and murmuring rill,
And fruitful field and breezy hill,
And all that else the wide world fill
Are vocal with His name.

The sky can still remember it,
The earliest Christmas morn,
When in the cold December
The Savior Christ was born;
And still in darkness clouded
And still in noonday light,
It feels its far depths crowded
With Angels fair and bright.

No star unfolds its glory,
No trumpet's wind is blown,
But tells the Christmas story
In music of its own.
No eager strife of mortals,
In busy fields or town,
But sees the open portals
Through which the Christ came down.

# Angels We Have Heard on Heard on High

TRADITIONAL FRENCH

1. An - gels we have heard on high, Sweet - ly sing - ing o'er the plains;
2. Shep - herds, why this ju - bi - lee? Why your joy - ous strains pro - long?
3. Come to Beth - le - hem, and see Him whose birth the an - gels sing;
4. See Him in a man - ger laid, Whom the choirs of an - gels praise;

And the moun - tains in re - ply, Ech - o back their joy - ous strains.
What the glad - some tid - ings be Which in - spire your heav'n - ly song?
Come, a - dore on bend - ed knee Christ the Lord, the new - born King.
Ma - ry, Jo - seph, lend your aid, While our hearts in love we raise.

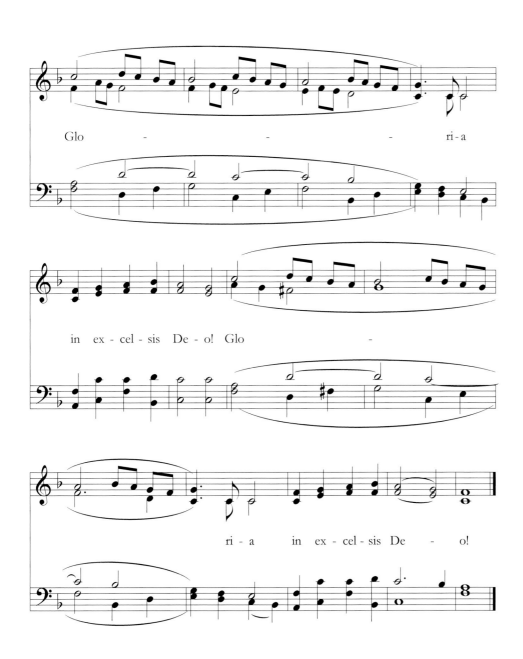

Glo - - - ri - a

in ex - cel - sis De - o! Glo -

ri - a in ex - cel - sis De - o!

# WE TOO ARE BIDDEN: THE SHEPHERD'S GIFT

Heywood Broun

They made haste to go to Bethlehem to see the thing which had come to pass. "For unto you," the angel said, "is born this day in the city of David a Saviour, which is Christ the Lord."

But as they journeyed to Bethlehem they fell into a discussion as to just how they should find the place where the infant lay. Indeed, one of the group grumbled, "In Bethlehem there be many mangers, and how are we to find the one?"

And the youngest shepherd said, "It will be made known to us."

The night was bright with stars and the way more easy than they had expected. The shepherds stood for a moment in some perplexity as to the appointed place.

And suddenly the volume of voices increased, and down the street there came a caravan of camels. Upon the backs of the beasts sat great bearded men, and with them they brought sacks of precious stuffs and huge treasure chests from distant kingdoms. The air was filled with the pungent tang of spice and perfume.

The startled shepherds stood against the wall to let the cavalcade of the mighty pass by. And these wise men and kings seemed to have no doubt as to their destination. They swept past the inn and dismounted at the door of a stable. Servants took the burdens from the backs of the camels, and the kings and the wise men stooped and went in through the low door of the stable.

"It is there the child lies in the manger," said one of the shepherds and made as if to follow, but his fellows were abashed and said among themselves, "It is not meet that we should crowd in upon the heels of the mighty."

"We, too, are bidden," insisted the youngest shepherd. "For us, as well, there was the voice of the angel of the Lord."

And timidly the men from the fields followed after and found places near the door. They watched as the men from distant countries came and silently placed their gifts at the foot of the manger where the child lay sleeping. And the shepherds stood aside and let the great of the earth go out into the night to take up again their long journey.

Presently they were alone, but as they had no gifts to lay beside the gold and frankincense they turned to go back to their flocks. But Mary, the mother, made a sign to the youngest shepherd to come closer. And he said, "We are shepherds, and we have come suddenly from the fields whence an angel summoned us. There is naught which we could add to the gifts of wise men and of kings."

Mary replied, "Before the throne of God, who is a king and who is a wise man, you have brought with you a gift more precious than all the others. It lies within your heart."

And suddenly it was made known to the shepherd the meaning of the words of Mary. He knelt at the foot of the manger and gave to the child his prayer of joy and of devotion.

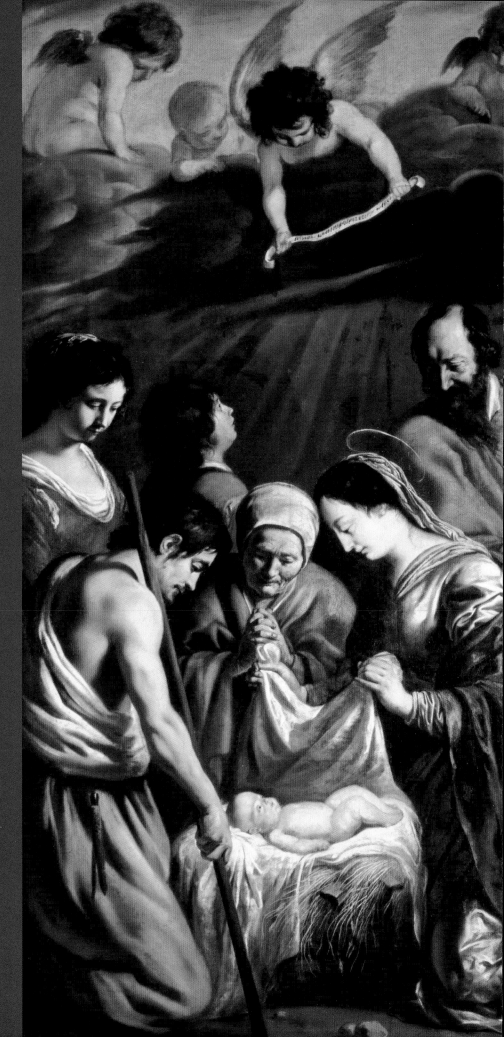

*Given, not
lent, but now
withdrawn
once sent, this
Infant of
mankind, this
One, is still
the little
welcome Son.*

—Alice Meynell

# Christmas

Faith Baldwin

The snow is full of silver light
Spilled from the heavens' tilted cup,
And on this holy, tranquil night,
The eyes of men are lifted up
To see the promise written fair,
The hope of peace for all on earth,
And hear the singing bells declare
The marvel of the dear Christ's birth.
The way from year to year is long
And though the road be dark so far,
Bright is the manger, sweet the song;
The steeple rises to the Star.

# What Means This Glory Round Our Feet?

James Russell Lowell

"What means this glory round our feet,"
The magi mused, "more bright than morn?"
And voices chanted clear and sweet,
"Today the Prince of Peace is born."

"What means that star," the shepherds said,
"That brightens through the rocky glen?"
And angels, answering overhead,
Sang, "Peace on earth, good will to men."

All round about our feet shall shine
A Light like that the wise men saw,
If we our loving wills incline
To that sweet life which is the law.

So shall we learn to understand
The simple faith of shepherds then,
And clasping kindly hand in hand,
Sing, "Peace on earth, good will to men."

And they who to their childhood cling
And keep at eve the faith of morn,
Shall daily hear the angels sing,
"Today the Prince of Peace is born."

*O star of wonder, star of night, Star with royal beauty bright, Westward leading, still proceeding, Guide us to thy perfect light.*
                              —John Henry Hopkins Jr.

# The Sending of the Magi
### Bliss Carman

In a far Eastern country it happened long of yore,
Where a lone and level sunrise flushes the desert floor,
That three kings sat together and a spearman kept the door.
Gaspar, whose wealth was counted by city and caravan;
With Melchior, the seer who read the starry plan;
And Balthasar, the blameless, who loved his fellow man.

There while they talked, a sudden strange rushing sound arose,
And as with startled faces they thought upon their foes,
Three figures stood before them in imperial repose.
One in flame-gold and one in blue and one in scarlet clear,
With the almighty portent of sunrise they drew near!
And the kings made obeisance with hand on breast, in fear.

"Arise," said they, "we bring you good tidings of great peace!
Today a power is wakened whose working must increase
Till fear and greed and malice and violence shall cease."
The messengers were Michael, by whom all things were wrought
To shape and hue; and Gabriel who is the lord of thought;
And Rafael without whose love all toil must come to nought.

Then while the kings' hearts greatened and all the chamber shone,
As when the hills at sundown take a new glory on
And the air thrills with purple, their visitors were gone.
Then straightway up rose Gaspar, Melchior, and Balthasar
And passed out through the murmur of palace and bazaar
To make without misgiving the journey of the Star.

# The Ballad of Befana
### Phyllis McGinley

Befana, the housewife, scrubbing her pane,
Saw three old sages ride down the lane,
Saw three gray travelers pass her door—
Gaspar, Balthazar, and Melchior.
"Where journey you, Sirs?" she asked of them.
And Gaspar answered, "To Bethlehem,
For we have news of a marvelous thing:
Born in a stable is Christ the King."

"Give Him my welcome!" Balthazar smiled,
"Come with us, Mistress, to greet the Child."
"Oh, happily, happily would I fare
Were my dusting through and I'd polished the stair."
Old Melchior leaned on his saddle horn.
"Then send but a gift to the small newborn."
"Oh, gladly, gladly I'd send Him one
Were my cupboards clean and my weaving done.
I'd give Him a robe to warm His sleep,
But first I must mend the fire and sweep.
As soon as ever I've baked my bread,
I'll fetch Him a pillow for His head
And a coverlet too," Befana said.
"When the rooms are aired and the line dry,
I'll look to the Babe." But the Three rode by.

She worked for a day and a night and a day,
Then, gifts in her hand, took up her way.
But she never could find where the Christ Child lay.
And still she wanders at Christmastide,
Houseless, whose house was all her pride,
Whose heart was tardy, whose gifts were late;
Wanders and knocks at every gate,
Crying, "Good people, the bells begin!
Put off your toiling and let love in!"

# AN ANGEL'S MESSAGE

Erma Ferrari

*I*n Jerusalem, where the magi had stopped to inquire for a newly born king, the aged and evil King Herod was alarmed. Was somebody challenging the right of the Herods to rule Judea? "Go and search diligently for the young child," he had told the wise men, "and bring me word, that I may come and worship him also." But the wise men were warned by God of Herod's trickery, and they returned home by another way.

And not long after the magi's visit, Joseph awoke one night from a troubled sleep. "Mary, God spoke to me in a dream, saying, 'Arise, and take the young child and his mother, and flee into Egypt.' We must leave Bethlehem at once, tonight."

Mary quickly gathered some household goods for Joseph to pack on the little donkey. God had spoken to Joseph and she must obey. She did not question the ways of God.

Silently, Joseph led the donkey through the darkness down the southern slope of the city. Beside him, Mary carried the baby.

"When Herod dies, we will return," Joseph said, as they hurried along the caravan route to Egypt.

But Mary and Joseph never returned to Bethlehem. When King Herod died, his equally cruel son, Archelaus, became king of Judea. God directed Joseph to take the young wife and child back to their first home in Nazareth, which lay in Galilee.

And Mary was glad, for in Galilee there were green fields for a growing boy to explore and gentle hills to climb.

*Christmas is a quest. May each of us follow his star of faith and find the heart's own Bethlehem.*
*—Esther Baldwin York*

The Gift of Glory

*For unto us a child is born, unto us a son is given: and the government shall be upon his shoulder: and his name shall be called Wonderful, Counsellor, The mighty God, The everlasting Father, The Prince of Peace.*
—*Isaiah 9:6*

# THE CHRISTMAS STORY

According to the Gospels of Luke and Matthew, KJV

And it came to pass in those days, that there went out a decree from Cæsar Augustus, that all the world should be taxed. And all went to be taxed, every one into his own city. And Joseph also went up from Galilee, out of the city of Nazareth, into Judæa, unto the city of David, which is called Bethlehem; (because he was of the house and lineage of David:) To be taxed with Mary his espoused wife, being great with child.

And so it was, that, while they were there, the days were accomplished that she should be delivered. And she brought forth her firstborn son, and wrapped him in swaddling clothes, and laid him in a manger; because there was no room for them in the inn.

And there were in the same country, shepherds abiding in the field, keeping watch over their flock by night. And lo, the angel of the Lord came upon them, and the glory of the Lord shone round about them: and they were sore afraid. And the angel said unto them, Fear not: for, behold, I bring you good tidings of great joy, which shall be to all people. For unto you is born this day in the city of David a Saviour, which is Christ the Lord. And this shall be a sign unto you; Ye shall find the babe wrapped in swaddling clothes, lying in a manger. And suddenly there was with the angel a multitude of the heavenly host praising God, and saying, Glory to God in the highest, and on earth peace, good will toward men.

And it came to pass, as the angels were gone away from them into heaven, the shepherds said one to another, Let us now go even unto Bethlehem, and see this thing which is come to pass, which the Lord hath made known unto us. And they came with haste, and found Mary, and Joseph, and the babe lying in a manger. And when they had seen it, they made known abroad the saying which was told them concerning this child. And all they that heard it wondered at those things which were told them by the shepherds.

Now when Jesus was born in Bethlehem of Judæa in the days of Herod the king, behold, there came wise men from the east to Jerusalem, saying, Where is he that is born King of the Jews? for we have seen his star in the east, and are come to worship him. When Herod the king had heard these things,

he was troubled, and all Jerusalem with him. And when he had gathered all the chief priests and scribes of the people together, he demanded of them where Christ should be born. And they said unto him, In Bethlehem of Judæa; for thus it is written by the prophet, And thou Bethlehem, in the land of Juda, art not the least among the princes of Juda: for out of thee shall come a Governor, that shall rule my people Israel.

Then Herod, when he had privily called the wise men, inquired of them diligently what time the star appeared. And he sent them to Bethlehem, and said, Go and search diligently for the young child; and when ye have found him, bring me word again, that I may come and worship him also. When they had heard the king, they departed; and lo, the star, which they saw in the east, went before them,

till it came and stood over where the young child was. When they saw the star, they rejoiced with exceeding great joy.

And when they were come into the house, they saw the young child with Mary his mother, and fell down and worshiped him: and when they had opened their treasures, they presented unto him gifts: gold, and frankincense and myrrh. And being warned of God in a dream that they should not return to Herod, they departed into their own country another way. And when they

were departed, behold, the angel of the Lord appeareth to Joseph in a dream, saying, Arise, and take the young child and his mother, and flee into Egypt, and be thou there until I bring thee word: for Herod will seek the young child to destroy him. When he arose, he took the young child and his mother by night, and departed into Egypt: And was there until the death of Herod: that it might be fulfilled which was spoken of the Lord by the prophet, saying, Out of Egypt have I called my son.

# THE GREATEST GIFT

George Hodges

Now, all that day, travelers had been journeying in unusual numbers along the ways which led to Bethlehem, for it was the time of a census. Caesar Augustus . . . wished to know how many people were living in that part of the country. . . . Every man had to go to his own city; that is, to the place in which his family belonged. So there was a great stir all about the land, with men going to this place and to that to have their names written in the census-books. Among the others, out of Nazareth came Joseph, the carpenter, because he was of the family of David, and with him Mary, his espoused wife, who was to be the mother of the King. Down they came like other poor folk, over hill and dale, till they arrived at Bethlehem. But when they reached the town there was no place where they might stay. Every house was full of guests, and the inn was already crowded. The only shelter was a stable—a common stable, strewn with hay, with dusty cobwebs hanging from the rafters, and occupied by cows and donkeys. There, accordingly, they went.

And there, while the angels sang and the sky blazed over the pastures of the sheep, the King came. The King of Glory came! The mighty God, the Maker of all things, the Lord most high, came to dwell among us. And behold, he was a little child. And Mary wrapped him warm in swaddling clothes, as the way is with babies, and laid him in the manger.

There the shepherds, all out of breath with running, found them—Mary and Joseph, and the babe lying in a manger. And they told what they had seen and heard about the singing angels and the King of Glory while Mary listened, remembering the angel who had appeared to her. So the shepherds returned, glorifying and praising God for all the wonders of that night. Thus was kept the first Christmas, with carols by the choir of heaven, and God's own Son, the Saviour of the world, coming as a Christmas gift for all mankind.

## A Mother's Reflection
### Kay Hoffman

Sweet little Babe in bed of straw,
Upon thy face I gaze with awe.
You truly are God's own dear Son,
Messiah, the long awaited one.
The shepherds come, Thee to adore
And humbly kneel on straw-strewn floor;

Magi, star-led o'er desert sand,
Have brought Thee jewels from a far land.
The oxen gaze with wondering eyes;

To them You are a sweet surprise.
Gentle doves draw near to coo
Their own soft lullaby to You.

My tiny Babe in bed of straw,
You are the Saviour born for all—
God's gift of love sent from on high.
Sleep, little one, till dawn draws nigh.
The whole world will Thy birth recall,
Messiah born in a stable stall.


## Christmas Prayer
### Gail Brook Burket

O Prince of Peace, come now to bless
The whole war-weary earth,
As long ago, when angel choirs
Were heralds of Thy birth.

Forgive us when we place our trust
In armament's mad force
And spurn almighty power which stays
The planets in their course.

Give us the will to use our lives
To serve the common good
That all the peoples of the earth
May know true brotherhood.

Oh, let Thy reign supplant the sword
And turn all hearts to Thee.
Thine is the love which conquers all
And Thine true victory.


*Celestial choirs from courts above,*
*Shed sacred glories there;*
*And angels with their sparkling lyres*
*Make music on the air.*
—*Edmund Hamilton Sears*

# MESSIAH

Jim Bishop

The fire outside burned brightly in the southerly breeze. Joseph sat beside it, heating the water and praying. No one came down from the inn to ask how the young woman felt. If she prayed, no one heard except the animals, some of whom stopped chewing for a moment to watch; others of whom opened sleepy eyes to see. The future of mankind hung in space.

Joseph had run out of prayers and promises. He looked up; three stars were fused into one tremendously bright one. His eyes caught the glint of bright blue light, almost like a tiny moon, and he wondered about it and was still vaguely troubled by it when he heard a tiny, thin wail, a sound so slender that one had to listen again for it to make sure. He wanted to rush inside at once. He got to his feet, and he moved no further. She would call him. He would wait.

"Joseph." It was a soft call, but he heard it. At once, he picked up the second jar of water and hurried inside. The two lamps still shed a soft glow over the stable, even though it seemed years since they had been lighted.

The first thing he noticed was his wife. Mary was sitting with her back against a manger wall. Her face was clean; her hair had been brushed. There were blue hollows under her eyes. She smiled at her husband and nodded. She beckoned him to come closer. Joseph, mouth agape, followed her to a little manger. It had been cleaned, but where the animals had nipped the edges of

the wood, the boards were worn and splintered. In the manger were the broad
bolts of white swaddling she had brought on the trip. They were doubled
underneath and over the top of the baby.

Mary smiled at her husband as he bent far over to look. There, among the
cloths, he saw the tiny red face of an infant. This, said Joseph to himself, is the
one of whom the angel spoke. He dropped to his knees beside the manger.
This was the Messiah.

# What Makes Christmas?

Author Unknown

"What is Christmas?"
I asked my soul,
And this answer
Came back to me:
"It is the
Glory of heaven come down
In the hearts of humanity—
Come in the spirit and heart of a Child,
And it matters not what we share
At Christmas; it is not Christmas at all
Unless the Christ Child be there."

# The Shepherds Had an Angel

Christina Rossetti

The shepherds had an angel,
The wise men had a star,
But what have I, a little child,
To guide me home from far,
Where glad stars sing together
And singing angels are?

The wise men left their country
To journey morn by morn,
With gold and frankincense and myrrh,
Because the Lord was born;
God sent a star to guide them
And sent a dream to warn.

My life is like their journey,
Their star is like God's book;
I must be like those good wise men

With heavenward heart and look.
But shall I give no gifts to God?
What precious gifts they took!

Lord, I will give my love to Thee,
Than gold much costlier,
Sweeter to Thee than frankincense,
More prized than choicest myrrh.
Lord, make me dearer day by day,
Day by day holier;

Nearer and dearer day by day;
Till I my voice unite
And sing my 'Glory, glory,'
With angels clad in white.
All 'Glory, glory,' given to Thee,
Through all the heavenly height.

# THE HOLY NIGHT

Selma Lagerlof

There was a man who went out in the dark night to borrow live coals to kindle a fire. He went from hut to hut and knocked. "Dear friends, help me!" said he. "My wife has just given birth to a child, and I must make a fire to warm her and the little one." But all the people were asleep. No one replied.

The man walked and walked. At last he saw the gleam of a fire a long way off. Then he went in that direction and saw that the fire was burning in the open. A lot of sheep were sleeping around the fire, and an old shepherd sat and watched over the flock.

When the man who wanted to borrow fire came up to the sheep, he saw that three big dogs lay asleep at the shepherd's feet. All three awoke when the man approached and opened their great jaws as though they wanted to bark, but not a sound was heard. The man noticed that the hair on their backs stood up and that their sharp, white teeth glistened in the firelight. They dashed toward him.

One of them bit at his leg and one at his hand and one clung to his throat. But their jaws and teeth wouldn't obey them, and the man didn't suffer harm.

Now the man wished to go farther, to get what he needed. But the sheep lay back to back and so close to one another that he couldn't pass them. Then the man stepped upon their backs and walked over them and up to the fire. And not one of the animals awoke or moved.

When the man had almost reached the fire, the shepherd looked up. He was a surly old man who was unfriendly and harsh toward human beings. And when he saw the strange man coming, he seized the long, spiked staff, which he always held in his hand when he tended his flock, and threw it at him. The staff came right toward the man, but, before it reached him, it turned off to one side and whizzed past him, far out in the meadow.

Now the man came up to the shepherd and said to him: "Good man, help me, and lend me a little fire! My wife has just given birth to a child, and I must make a fire to warm her and the little one."

The shepherd would rather have said no, but when he pondered that the dogs couldn't hurt the man, the sheep had not run from him, and the staff had not wished to strike him, he was afraid and dared not deny the man.

"Take as much as you need!" he said to the man.

But then the fire was nearly burnt out. There were no logs or branches left, only a big heap of live coals; and the stranger had neither spade nor shovel wherein he could carry the red-hot coals.

When the shepherd saw this, he said again: "Take as much as you need!" And he was glad that the man wouldn't be able to take away any coals.

But the man stooped and picked coals from the ashes with his bare hands and laid them in his mantle. And he didn't burn his hands when he touched them, nor did the coals scorch his mantle; but he carried them away as if they had been nuts or apples.

And when the shepherd, who was such a cruel and hardhearted man, saw all this, he began to wonder to himself: What kind of a night is this, when the dogs do not bite, the sheep are not scared, the staff does not kill, or the fire scorch? He called the stranger back and said to him: "What kind of a night is this? And how does it happen that all things show you compassion?"

Then said the man: "I cannot tell you if you do not see it." And he wished to go his way, that he might soon make a fire and warm his wife and child.

But the shepherd did not wish to lose sight of the man before he had found out what all this might portend. He got up and followed the man till they came to the place where he lived.

Then the shepherd saw that the man didn't have so much as a hut to dwell in, but that his wife and babe were lying in a mountain grotto, where there was nothing except the cold and naked stone walls.

But the shepherd thought that perhaps the poor innocent child might freeze to death there in the grotto; and, although he was a hard man, he was touched and thought he would like to help it. And he loosened his knapsack from his shoulder, took from it a soft white sheepskin, gave it to the strange man, and said that he should let the child sleep on it.

But just as soon as he showed that he, too, could be merciful, his eyes were opened, and he saw what he had not been able to see before and heard what he could not have heard before.

He saw that all around him stood a ring of little silver-winged angels, and each held a stringed instrument, and all sang in loud tones that tonight the Saviour was born who should redeem the world from its sins.

Then he understood how all things were so happy this night that they didn't want to do anything wrong.

And it was not only around the shepherd that there were angels, but he saw them everywhere. They sat inside the grotto, they sat outside on the mountain, and they flew under the heavens. They came marching in great companies, and, as they passed, they paused and cast a glance at the child.

There were such jubilation and such gladness and songs and play! And all this he saw in the dark night, whereas before he could not have made out anything. He was so happy because his eyes had been opened that he fell upon his knees and thanked God.

What that shepherd saw we might also see, for the angels fly down from heaven every Christmas Eve, if we could only see them.

You must remember this, for it is as true, as true as that I see you and you see me. It is not revealed by the light of lamps or candles, and it does not depend upon sun and moon; but that which is needful is that we have such eyes as can see God's glory.

# *As with Gladness Men of Old*

William C. Dix

As with gladness men of old
Did the guiding star behold;
As with joy they hailed its light,
Leading onward, beaming bright;
So, most gracious Lord, may we
Evermore your splendor see.

As with joyful steps they sped
To that lowly manger bed,
There to bend the knee before
Christ whom heaven and earth adore;
So may we with hurried pace
Run to seek your throne of grace.

As they offered gifts most rare
At that manger crude and bare;
So may we this holy day,
Drawn to you without delay,
All our costliest treasures bring,
Christ, to you, our heavenly King.

Christ Redeemer, with us stay,
Help us live your holy way;
And when earthly things are past,
Bring our ransomed souls at last
Where they need no star to guide,
Where no clouds your glory hide.

In the heavenly city bright
None shall need created light;
You, its light, its joy, its crown,
You, its sun which goes not down;
There for ever may we sing
Alleluias to our King.

## Before the Paling of the Stars

Christina G. Rossetti

Before the paling of the stars,
    Before the winter morn,
Before the earliest cockcrow,
    Jesus Christ was born—
Born in a stable,
    Cradled in a manger,
In the world His hands had made,
    Born a stranger.

Priest and king lay fast asleep
    In Jerusalem;
Young and old lay fast asleep
    In crowded Bethlehem.
Saint and Angel, ox and ass,
    Kept a watch together
Before the Christmas daybreak
    In the winter weather.

Jesus on His mother's breast
    In the stable cold,
Spotless Lamb of God was He,
    Shepherd of the fold.
Let us kneel with Mary maid,
    With Joseph bent and hoary,
With Saint and Angel, ox and ass,
    To hail the King of Glory.

*"What is Christmas?" I asked my soul, and this answer came back to me: "It is the glory of heaven come down in the hearts of humanity."* —Author Unknown

# O Come, All Ye Faithful

JOHN FRANCIS WADE

1. O    come, all ye   faith - ful,   joy - ful and tri - um-phant,
2.      Sing, choirs of   an - gels,   sing in ex - ul  - ta - tion!
3.      Child, for us   sin - ners   poor and in the   man - ger,
4.      Yea, Lord, we   greet Thee,   born this hap - py   morn-ing,

O   come ye, O   come   ye to   Beth  - le - hem!
O   sing,  all ye  cit - i - zens of  heav'n   a - bove;
    we   would em - brace   Thee with  love   and  awe;
Je - sus, to  Thee   be  all  glo  - ry   given;

Come and be - hold Him, born the King of an - gels;
"Glo - ry to God, all glo - ry in the high - est;"
Who would not love Thee, lov - ing us so dear - ly?
Word of the Fa - ther, now in flesh ap - pear - ing;

O come, let us a - dore Him, O come, let us a - dore Him,

O come, let us a - dore Him, Christ the Lord.

# CHRISTMAS ANGEL

Pamela Kennedy

Celestin knew the time was nearing. Not because time mattered to him, but because it was important to Majesty. When the fullness of time arrived, Celestin wanted to be ready to obey instantly. Obedience was the highest service among the angels. It was their never-ending gift to Majesty.

Celestin often pondered the way obedience seemed so difficult for humans. He didn't understand that. Limited as they were by time and space, it seemed only logical that they would want to experience life on earth to the fullest. After all, their days were brief. Couldn't they see that Majesty knew best? He spoke His eternal wisdom to them in nature, whispered it to them through their souls, wrote it in His Word, and shouted it through His prophets. Still they resisted. Now, in an act of grace and mercy Celestin could not comprehend, Majesty was sending the Only Begotten to these stiff-necked creatures. Surely now, they would finally learn obedience and experience the richness of living according to their Maker's will.

It had been almost a year in earth time since Gabriel traveled to Nazareth to speak to Mary. Celestin understood why she had been chosen. He had watched as Gabriel told the young maiden of Majesty's plan. Despite her troubled questions, she had bowed her head in humble obedience and said, "I am the Lord's servant. May it be to me as you have said." Oh, how the angelic choir had rejoiced at that moment! Celestin could still hear the chords of praise echoing in the eternal reaches of heaven.

Celestin wondered how Majesty would introduce the Only Begotten to the world. Perhaps it would be in a mighty temple with row upon row of priests praising God and blowing trumpets. Maybe there would be a tremendous earthquake or tidal wave presaging the event. Majesty used pillars of fire and parted water when he helped Moses, but Celestin felt sure there would be something more magnificent and wonderful for the Only Begotten. He would have to wait and see. Impatience was not becoming of an angel.

When the call came, it was not at all what Celestin had expected. He was to take a multitude of angels and travel to a dark hillside outside a little town called Bethlehem. There he was to make an announcement to a small group of poor men tending a flock of sheep. He was to say: "Do not be afraid. I bring you good news of great joy that will be for all people. Today in the town of David a Saviour has been born to you; he is Christ the Lord. This will be a sign to you; you will find a baby wrapped in cloths and lying in a manger." At that point, he was to lead his fellow angels in choruses of praise to God.

"Are you sure that's it?" Celestin asked the messenger from the Throne. "No temple or palace or parted seas or comet shower or anything?"

The other angel shook his head. Then he raised his hand as if remembering something. "Oh, there will be a star," he added.

"A star?" Celestin repeated incredulously. "Just one star?"

"Yes," the messenger repeated with a sigh, "just one star—over a little animal shelter, behind an inn, on a back alley in Bethlehem."

"With all due respect," Celestin continued, "do you think you could have misunderstood the message? We're talking about the Only Begotten here, the Creator, the Sustainer, the Holy One."

The other angel squared his shoulders and looked just a bit perturbed. "That is the message as Majesty gave it to me. I do not question Him." He vanished, leaving Celestin alone and stinging from the mild rebuke.

"Well, I only asked," he muttered. "I wasn't planning to disobey!"

Quickly he summoned a company of angels and led them to the assigned hillside. The shepherds fell on the ground and quaked, just as Celestin had known they would. Humans were always so discomfited by the sight of angels. He reassured them then with Majesty's words and led the angelic choir as they sang, "Glory to God in the highest, and on earth peace to men." He would have preferred something with more hallelujahs, but that wasn't in the orders for tonight.

When the angelic chorus ended and the others returned to heaven, Celestin remained behind. He wanted to see the Only Begotten. He still could not fathom why Majesty had chosen such a homely way to introduce such magnificence.

Silently Celestin hovered in the shadows of the tiny stable. The silver light of one pure star softly illuminated the stony walls. Mary, the obedient one, and Joseph, her loving husband, reclined on the straw. In her arms, she held an infant wrapped in swaddling cloths. Could this be the Only Begotten—here, in these rude surroundings? It was unthinkable. Celestin recalled the dazzling light originating from Majesty's throne, the myriad angels constantly in attendance, the never-ending praises attending His presence. And then he gazed once more at the little family surrounded only by sleeping cows and sheep.

Suddenly, a solitary word flashed into Celestin's mind with brilliant clarity: love. Here in this humble setting, Majesty had spoken it not with thunder or earthquake, nor with an angelic chorus or even a single trumpet blast, but with flesh and blood. The Only Begotten had left the glories of heaven to bring true love to humanity. Here in this tiny town it would begin, but Celestin knew such love could never be confined. Time or space, even eternity, would not be sufficient to contain such abundance. It would flow like a river watering the souls of generation after generation of earth's citizens. A twinge of envy touched Celestin's heart as he realized even an angel could never know such joy as this. He bowed then in reverence before the tiny one lying in Mary's arms, and a gentle breeze brushed the Baby's cheek as the angel whispered, "Holy, Holy, Holy."

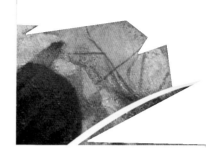

## The Risk of Birth
Madeleine L'Engle

This is no time for a child to be born,
With the earth betrayed by war and hate
And a nova lighting the sky to warn
That time runs out and sun burns late.

That was no time for a child to be born,
In a land in the crushing grip of Rome;
Honour and truth were trampled by scorn—
Yet here did the Saviour make His home.

When is the time for love to be born?
The inn is full on the planet earth,
And by greed and pride the sky is torn—
Yet Love still takes the risk of birth.

## A Christmas Gift
### Clarence Hawkes

A Christmas gift Love sends to thee,
'Tis not a gift that you may see,
Like frankincense or shining gold;
Yet 'tis a gift that you may hold.

If you are lacking bread and meat,
'Twill give you heavenly bread to eat;
If you are down-trod, e'en as Job,
'Twill dress you in a seamless robe.

The gift of love in Mary's eyes
Looked down on Jesus with surprise,
That One so great should be so small,
To point the way for kings and all.

One heart of love can move the race;
One grain of truth can change earth's face:
A Bethlehem Babe, a shepherd's rod
Have lifted mankind up to God.

## Christmas Day
### Philip Doddridgea

Hark, the glad sound! the Saviour comes,
The Saviour promised long;
Let every heart prepare a throne
And every voice a song!

He comes, the broken heart to bind,
The bleeding soul to cure,
And with the treasures of His grace
To enrich the humble poor.

Our glad Hosannas, Prince of Peace,
Thy welcome shall proclaim,
And heaven's eternal arches ring
With Thy beloved name.

# TITLE INDEX

# AUTHOR INDEX

# ACKNOWLEDGMENTS

*(continued from page 4)* BISHOP, JIM. "Messiah" from *The Day Christ Was Born.* Copyright © 1960 by Jim Bishop and renewed 1988 by Betty Kelly Bishop. Reprinted by permission of HarperCollins Publishers, Inc. BRUN, MARCEL and BOWEN, BETTY. "The Tailor's Christmas Guest" from *The Shining Tree and Other Christmas Stories,* edited by Hildegard Hawthorne and Marcel Brun. Copyright © 1940. DREDLA, ALBERTA. "Christmas Gifts." Used by permission of the author. EVANS, COLLEEN TOWNSEND. "What Shall We Do This Christmas?" from *The Meaning of Christmas.* Edited by Phyllis Hobe. Copyright © 1975 by the editor. Published by A. J. Holman Co./J. B. Lippincott/HarperCollins. FERRARI, ERMA. "An Angel's Message" from *The Life of Jesus of Nazareth* by Erma Ferrari. Copyright © 1958 by Simon and Schuster, Inc. and Artists and Writers Guild, Inc. GUEST, EDGAR A. "A Kindled Flame of Love." Used by permission of Henry Sobell, Jr. HAZELTINE, ALICE ISABEL. "Christmas Roses" from *The Christmas Book of Legends and Stories* by Elva Sophronia Smith and Alice Isabel Hazeltine. Copyright © 1944 by Lothrop, Lee and Shepherd, Co., NY. L'ENGLE, MADELINE. "The Risk of Birth" from *A Treasury of Christmas Classics.* Copyright © 1994 by Harold Shaw Publishers, Wheaton, IL. LERNET-HOLENIA, ALEXANDER. "The Three Wise Men of Totenleben," translated by Judith Bernays Heller, from *Christmas Is Here.* Edited by Anne Fremantle. Copyright © 1955 by the Stephen Daye Press. LOGAN, BEN. "The Year the Presents Didn't Come" from *Christmas Remembered.* Copyright © 1997 by Ben Logan. Published by NorthWord Press. MCGINLEY, PHYLLIS. "The Ballad of Befana." Copyright © 1957 by Phyllis McGinley. Reprinted by permission of Curtis Brown Ltd. SMALL, MARY. "Christmas and Peter Moss" from *Star of Wonder: Christmas Stories and Poems for Children.* Collected by Pat Alexander. Copyright © 1996 by Pat Alexander. Lion Publishing, London. Our sincere thanks to the following authors whom we were unable to locate: Heywood Broun for "We Too, Are Bidden"; Mary Ellen Chase for "Late for Christmas"; The Estate of Ralph Spaulding Cushman for "Christmas Prayer"; Clarence Hawkes for "A Christmas Gift"; Pat Corrick Hinton for "Prayer at Christmas"; Laurie Lee for "Carols in the Cotswolds"; The Estate of William P. Remington for "The Keeper of the Inn."

All possible care has been taken to fully acknowledge the ownership and use of every selection in this book. If any mistakes or omissions have occurred, they will be corrected in subsequent editions, provided notification is sent to the publisher.

# PHOTOGRAPHS

Cover, Snow-covered trees in Willard Brook State Forest, Townsend, Massachusetts, © William Johnson; 1-2 Beached glacial ice in Muir Inlet, Glacier Bay National Park, Alaska, © Carr Clifton; 4-5 Sunset over the Teton Range, Grand Teton National Park, Wyoming, © Carr Clifton; 6-7 Snow on the banks of the Ammonoosuc River at sunrise over Twin Mountain, Bethlehem, New Hampshire, © William H. Johnson; 8-9 Antique musical instruments and candles, © Jessie Walker; 11 Homemade holiday treats, © Jessie Walker; 12-13 Cottage decorated for Christmas, © Jessie Walker; 14-15 *WIND CHILL* by Karl J. Kuerner III, © Superstock; 18-19 *SCHOOL'S OUT* by Samuel S. Carr, © Christie's Images; 22 Door decorated for Christmas, © Jessie Walker; 26 Lighted log cottages in Colorado snow, © Superstock; 29 Snow-covered hill in Maine, © Superstock; 30-31 Snowy trees and field, © Superstock; 32-33 *UNTRODDEN SNOW WITHIN THREE MILES OF CHARING CROSS, HOLLAND PARK* by Andrew McCallum © Christie's Images; 34-35 *A DUTCH VILLAGE IN WINTER* by Willem Koekkoek, © Christie's Images; 38-39 *GOING TO CHURCH* by Hermann Kaufmann, © Christie's Images; 41 *A WINTER BOUQUET* by Harry Van Der Weyden, © Christie's Images; 44-45 *A CAPRICCO VIEW OF A TOWN WITH FIGURES ON A FROZEN CANAL* by Jan Hendrik Verheyen, © Christie's Images; 49 *L'HIVER A MONTFOUCAULT (EFFET DE NEIGE)* by Camille Pissarro, © Christie's Images; 50 Baskets of vegetables on table with candles, © Jessie Walker; 52-53 Sun streaming through snow-covered trees, © Superstock; 54 *L'EGLISE DE JEUFOSSE, TEMPS DE NEIGE* by Claude Monet, © Christie's Images; 57 Snow-covered fir tree with lights and ornaments at dusk in Bristol, New Hampshire, © William H. Johnson; 58-59 *NURSEMAIDS, HIGH BRIDGE PARK* by George Luks, © Christie's Images; 63 *THE CHRISTMAS TREE* by Elizabeth Adela Stanhope, © Christie's Images; 67 Lighted church at dusk in a New England Town, © Superstock; 68-69 *MILLSTREAM IN NEW EPSWICH, NEW HAMPSHIRE* by William Jurian Kaula, © Superstock; 72-73 Antique Christmas card, © Fine Art Photographic Library Ltd.; 74-75 Winter sun in the Shawangunk Mountains of New York, © Carr Clifton; 76-77 Peaks above Saint Mary Lake, Glacier National Park, Montana, © Carr Clifton; 78 Snow-covered fir trees on Old Speck Mountain, Grafton Notch State Park, Maine, © William H. Johnson; 80-81 *TIMES SQUARE, WINTER IN NEW YORK* by Guy Carleton Wiggins, © Christie's Images; 84-85 Winter landscape in North Kingstown, Rhode Island, © Superstock; 86-87 *WINTERLANDSCHAFT MIT KIRCHE* by Caspar David Friedrich, © Christie's Images; 90-91 *CHRISTMAS CHEER* by George Sheridan Knowles, © Christie's Images; 94-95 *TWILIGHT IN GLOUCESTER* by Paul Cornoyer, © Christie's Images; 96-97 Fir tree in the snow decorated for the season, © William H. Johnson; 98-99 Snow-covered trees on a sunny winter day, © Superstock; 100-101 Christmas tree decorated with apples and cookies, © Jessie Walker; 103 Winter landscape at sunset, © Superstock; 104-105 Sunset on Saint Mary Lake, Glacier National Park, Montana, © Carr Clifton; 107 Sunrise over Cape Hatteras National Seashore, North Carolina, © Carr Clifton; 108 *MUSIC-MAKING ANGEL WITH LUTE* by Melozzo da Forli, © Superstock; 111 *THE WINTER SHEPHERD* by Daniel Sherrin, © Fine Art Photographic Library Ltd.; 114-115 *ADORATION OF THE SHEPHERDS* by Francesco Zuccarelli, © Superstock; 119 Two angels by Unknown Artist, © Fine Arts Photographic Library Ltd.; 120-121 *ADORATION OF THE SHEPHERDS* by Louis Le Nain, © Superstock; 122-123 *THE NATIVITY* by Gari Melchers, © Superstock; 124-125 *A FROZEN WINTER LANDSCAPE* by Johannes Bartholomaus Duntze, © Christie's Images; 127 *TOBIOLO AND THE ANGEL* detail by Giovanni Girolamo Savoldo, © Superstock; 128-129 Hemlock tree trunks covered with snow at sunrise, Wompatuck State Park, Massachusetts, © William H. Johnson; 130-131 *AN ANGEL* by John Melhuish Strudwick, © Christie's Images; 132-133 *FLIGHT INTO EGYPT* by Gysbrecht Leytens, © Fine Art Photographic Library Ltd.; 134 *ADORATION OF THE SHEPHERDS* by Domenico Zampieri Domenichino, © Fine Art Photographic Library Ltd.; 136-137 *THE BIRTH OF CHRIST* by Abraham Bloomaert, © Superstock; 138-139 *THE MADONNA AND CHILD IN GLORY WITH CHERUBS* by Giovanni Battista Salvi, il Sassoferrato, © Christie's Images; 141 Sunset over the Androscoggin River Valley, Bethel, Maine, © William H. Johnson; 144-145 *THE HOLY FAMILY* by Luca Giordano, © Fine Art Photographic Library Ltd.; 146-147 *THE ADORATION OF THE SHEPHERDS* attributed to Willem Van Herp, © Christie's Images; 148 The Pemigewasset River and Falls in Franconia Notch State Park, New Hampshire, © William H. Johnson; 152 *ANGELS AND HOLY CHILD* by Marianne Stokes, © Fine Art Photographic Library Ltd.; 156-157 Snow-capped peaks of the Grand Tetons, Montana, © Terry Donnelly.